The Cocos (Keeling) Islands

The Cocos (Keeling) Islands

Australian Atolls in the Indian Ocean

Pauline Bunce

The Jacaranda Press

First published 1988 by
THE JACARANDA PRESS
33 Park Road, Milton, Qld 4064
for THE COCOS (KEELING) ISLANDS COUNCIL

Typeset in 10/13 pt Rockwell Light

Printed in Singapore

National Library of Australia
Cataloguing-in-Publication data

Bunce, Pauline.
  The Cocos (Keeling) Islands.

  Includes index.
  ISBN 0 7016 2457 4.

  1. Cocos (Keeling) Islands — History. 2. Cocos (Keeling)
  Islands — Social life and customs. I. Title.

969'.9

Designed by Carolyn Morgan Design Studio

All photographs are the work of the author,
unless otherwise indicated.

This publication has been funded by
The Australian Bicentennial Authority
to celebrate Australia's Bicentenary
in 1988.

Australia
1788-1988

Cover photograph: Pulu Maria
from West Island

To Nek Bika, Nek Renja
and the Cocos Community

ACKNOWLEDGEMENTS

The author acknowledges with gratitude the assistance, inspiration and encouragement given by many people. Special thanks is extended to: The Australian Bicentennial Authority; Patrick Armstrong, University of W.A.; Australian National Parks and Wildlife Service; Australian Government Information Service; Cocos (Keeling) Islands Administration; Cocos (Keeling) Islands Council and Cooperative Society; Cocos Bicentennial Committee; Colonial Office, London; Ken Chan; Churchill Photographics, Perth; Letty Clunies-Ross; Professor de Crusz and Henry de Sylva, Kandy, Sri Lanka; Commonwealth Department of Aviation; Commonwealth Department of Territories; Andrew Grant; Jack, Geoff and Liz Hand; Lee Hammond; John Hunt; Michael Hunt; Theo Huoy; David Hutchison; Imperial War Museum, London; Ross Jones; Dick and Christina Whittington; Kevron Photographics, Perth; Kodak Australasia; Lloyds of London; Phil McCulloch; Bob and Martha Morrow; Richard Mathews; Nek Bika (Bynie bin Satar), Nek Renja (Lauder bin Atlas) and the Cocos Malay community; National Library, Canberra; National Library, Singapore; National Mapping, Canberra; Royal Air Force veterans, Alan de Groot and John Hyde, England; Royal Australian Air Force; Carolyn Stuart; Cathy and Kris Sudharsana; Bill Syrette; Peter Travers-Laney, Cable and Wireless Company Archives, London; United Nations Organisation; David Williams; West Australian Newspapers Ltd.; Colin Woodroffe, The Australian National University, Canberra; Audrey Webb; numerous members of the West Island community, Cocos (Keeling) Islands; the Principal and Staff of West Island School; my Apple Macintosh computer and my Zodiac inflatable boat.

THE AUTHOR

Pauline Bunce first went to the Cocos (Keeling) Islands as a high school teacher in 1982 and became totally fascinated by the unique culture of the Cocos Malay people. She proceeded to learn the local Malay dialect and has spent countless hours with community elders recording historical events, religious practices and island customs.

A geographer by training, Miss Bunce has travelled widely in India and South-east Asia. She holds a Masters degree in Education in Developing Countries and is a Fellow of the Royal Geographical Society and of the Royal Anthropological Institute.

She has written for a number of magazines and has produced a booklet entitled "Cocos Malay Culture" for the Australian Department of Territories. When she is not travelling or working in Asia, Pauline Bunce is a resident of Western Australia.

Photo [L to R]: Nek Renja (Lauder bin Atlas), the author, Nek Bika (Bynie bin Satar).

CONTENTS

Sir Ninian and Lady Stephen
are welcomed to Cocos by
Yean binte Yapat, 1984
(*Courtesy Australian
Government Information
Service*)

FOREWORD

Of all Australia's inhabited Territories perhaps the most unusual and certainly the most distant and least known to most Australians are the Cocos (Keeling) Islands. These two coral atolls lie far out in the Indian Ocean, over 3600 km due west of Darwin.

It was only a little over 30 years ago that the islands became a territory of Australia, and it was only in 1984 that its permanent population, the Cocos Malay people, in an historic Act of Self-Determination witnessed by a United Nations Mission, voted overwhelmingly for political, social and economic integration with Australia. Since then the Territory has entered into the mainstream of life as an integral part of Australia.

The Cocos Malay people form a devoutly Islamic community and speak their own version of the "trading Malay" language of the old East Indies. They have successfully preserved a culture which is very much their own. Their history is a fascinating one, as is that of their island home. Until they came to it in the last century, the Cocos group of islands were true desert islands in the Robinson Crusoe sense of being entirely uninhabited, other than by great colonies of birds.

It is time that we became more familiar with this small group of fellow Australians, many of whom have now successfully settled in the towns and cities of Western Australia.

Australia's Bicentenary is an entirely appropriate time for the publication of this account of the people of this most western outpost of our nation.

His Excellency the Right Honorable
Sir Ninian Stephen AK, GCMG, GCVO, KBE,
Governor-General of Australia

A drop in the ocean

A tear-drop shaped coral atoll in the centre of the Indian Ocean, an opal in a sea of deepest blue, a tiny 14 sq km of land — truly, just a "drop in the ocean".

A diary entry by the author on first arrival at Cocos, 26 January 1982.

Most Australians have yet to fully appreciate the vast presence of the Indian Ocean which laps our western doorstep. Atlases have tended to neglect it as a region, yet it has considerable geographical, cultural and historical unity. The Indian Ocean region has had an important influence on the course of Australia's ancient and not so ancient history. This huge oceanic basin is the economic base for over half of the world's population, it has cradled a number of huge ancient civilisations and it has witnessed the development of three major world religions. Until now, most Australians have tended to identify with the Pacific Ocean region, to look to the islands with whom we share a common colonial background. These eastern neighbours of ours are mostly Christian, English-speaking and, until recently, have been relatively free of political unrest.

The Australian Bicentenary is an appropriate time for all Australians to re-examine the geographical position of our nation in the Southern Hemisphere, and to look more closely at our increasingly important links with the Indian Ocean and its people.

Australia owns two external territories in the Indian Ocean, Christmas Island and the Cocos (Keeling) Islands, yet relatively few Australians know much about them. The unusual name of the Cocos group has been created to avoid confusion with a number of other 'Cocos Islands' that exist around the world. These tiny specks of limestone and coral in the centre of a vast ocean may appear to be insignificant, merely a 'drop in the ocean' — yet their tiny size belies their strategic importance to Australia.

Unlike the Pacific, the Indian Ocean is not blessed with a large number of inhabited islands. Those that do exist are home to some 28 million people. These islands provide

invaluable contact points for international aircraft, and shipping, and vital meteorological information for Australian weather forecasting. The islands of the Indian Ocean are even more important from a geo-political point of view. This is reflected in the increasing international interest being shown in the region by the major world powers.

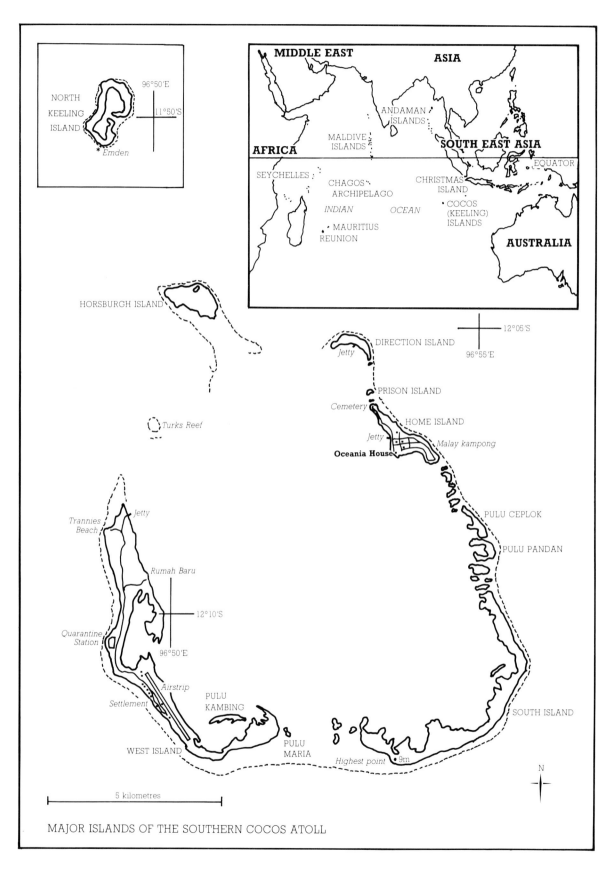

NORTH
KEELING
ISLAND

96°50'E

11°50'S

Emden

MIDDLE EAST

ASIA

ANDAMAN
ISLANDS

AFRICA

MALDIVE
ISLANDS

SOUTH EAST ASIA

EQUATOR

SEYCHELLES

CHAGOS
ARCHIPELAGO

CHRISTMAS
ISLAND

INDIAN   OCEAN

COCOS
(KEELING)
ISLANDS

MAURITIUS

REUNION

AUSTRALIA

HORSBURGH ISLAND

DIRECTION ISLAND

12°05'S

Jetty

96°55'E

PRISON ISLAND

Cemetery

HOME ISLAND

○ *Turks Reef*

Jetty

Malay kampong

Oceania House

PULU CEPLOK

PULU PANDAN

Jetty

*Trannies
Beach*

Rumah Baru

12°10'S

*Quarantine
Station*

96°50'E

Airstrip

Settlement

PULU
KAMBING

SOUTH ISLAND

WEST ISLAND

PULU
MARIA

Highest point • 9m

N

5 kilometres

MAJOR ISLANDS OF THE SOUTHERN COCOS ATOLL

Over the last century and a half the Cocos-Keeling atoll has provided both backdrop and stage for a great many dramas of the human spirit. It was here that the Royal Australian Navy had its first encounter with an enemy warship. The elusive German raider, *SMS Emden*, was shelled, driven aground and battered into surrender by the *HMAS Sydney* in Cocos waters in 1914. It was from here that the Allies had planned to mount a large-scale counter-attack on the Japanese in 1945. It was to here that a United Nations mission was called when allegations of 'slavery' and 'feudalism' hit world headlines in 1972. In 1980 the Cocos Islanders attained the long-overdue, but embarrassing, distinction of being the last people in the world to be granted access to compulsory education.

These events have each provided full-length, well-publicised and widely reviewed dramas, acted out here in front of a world-wide audience. In addition to these full-scale performances, however, there have been countless smaller pieces enacted on the Cocos stage that have never been acclaimed and remain totally unrecorded. Their players were unknown, their stories deemed insignificant and any publicity was actively discouraged.

One of the major aims of this book is to rebuild and re-examine the Cocos 'theatre' - the islands and the environment that they presented to their early settlers. This book also endeavours to uncover as many of the unknown 'players' and forgotten 'manuscripts' as possible by recording a significant number of local events for the very first time. I hope that this publication will create an opportunity for all Australians to meet and applaud the countless unsung heroes and heroines who have passed across the Cocos stage during its 162 years of human settlement.

History has already recorded much about the islands' founder, Alexander Hare, and the subsequent settlement by the Clunies-Ross family. This book attempts to look beyond these larger-than-life characters to the islands themselves, their living environment and the countless anonymous individuals whose blood and sweat have made them what they are today. The unique customs and culture developed on these islands by the descendants of slaves and convicts speaks most highly of the strength of the human will to overcome servitude and give rise to a new identity.

This book is a mere drop in the ocean when it comes to a complete study of the Cocos-Keeling atoll. Each of the following chapters could well be developed into a volume of its own. I sincerely hope that these pages will stimulate others to investigate Australia's Indian Ocean outposts further, and I trust that many Cocos Malay youngsters will find a challenge here to learn more about their unique community and its often tragic history.

The dedication of this Bicentennial project to two favorite Cocos Malay elders is also a mere 'drop' in the vast ocean of gratitude that I owe to the Cocos Malay community. I have been shown so much generosity, warmth and honesty by these people since I first came here in 1982, that I have pledged the entire proceeds from the sale of this book to their community.

Nek Bika (Bynie bin Satar) and Nek Renja (Lauder bin Atlas) are National Living Treasures. Neither gentleman has had the opportunity to learn to read or write, but their mutual storehouse of wisdom and island memories is absolutely priceless. I have been exceedingly privileged to have learned the Cocos Malay language under their tutelage and to have shared their company on so many occasions. I am truly humbled by their faith in me to record their memoirs for future generations and I thank them deeply for the indelible impression that they have made on my life.

I only wish that they could live forever.

Pauline Bunce
Cocos 1988

Isolated Atolls

1

*We look at it on the map and it's a tiny pinpoint
in a blue waste called the Indian Ocean . . . we
catch ourselves wondering how a plane could
ever seek out and find that lone microcosm
holding its own against the greedy, encircling
dominion of the sea.*

**Coralie Rees, Qantas passenger
to Cocos, 1956**

The Cocos (Keeling) Islands are an Australian
Territory located in the Indian Ocean at latitude 12° 10′ S and longitude 96° 50′ E. They
lie 2768 km north-west of Perth and
3685 km almost due west of Darwin. Their
nearest neighbours are Christmas Island
(approximately 900 km NNE), and Sumatra and
Java (approximately 1000 km NE). It would be
hard to imagine a more remote piece of land
anywhere else on earth.

GEOLOGY

Almost all isolated oceanic islands such as
Cocos are sitting atop the remains of ancient
volcanic activity. The floors of the world's
oceans are littered with hills, valleys and
mountain ranges that easily rival many of the
features found on dry land. The Cocos
(Keeling) Islands are two coral atolls which
have developed on top of old volcanic seamounts, rising from a depth of 5000 m in the
north-eastern Indian Ocean.

   Bathymetric research shows that the islands'
foundations are actually two of a series of
undersea features known as the Vening
Meinesz Seamounts. This range of mountains
also takes in Christmas Island and extends in
a north-easterly direction from a prominent
seafloor feature of the Indian Ocean known as
the Ninetyeast Ridge. The Cocos atolls are two
peaks in a section of the range known as the
Cocos Rise. They are themselves connected
by a narrow underwater bank at a depth of
some 700–800 m. Approximately 150 km to the
south-west of Cocos lies another seamount,

known as Umitaka Mary, which rises to a point
only 16 m below the surface of the ocean.

   Taken as a series from Umitaka Mary in the
south-west to Christmas Island in the north-
east, this chain of seamounts provides a per-
fect example of the sequence of events that
leads to the formation of coral atolls and
oceanic islands. Over the last 100 million
years, the section of the earth's crust known
as the Indo-Australian Plate has been moving
steadily in a northerly direction towards the

deep chasm of the Java Trench. Along the way it has passed over a plume, or 'hot spot', where a column of molten material rises from deep in the mantle to produce a chain of seamounts in the overlying crust. The oldest of this family, Christmas Island, now uplifted and tilting back, is in the process of 'climbing' the crustal bulge that heralds the edge of the Java Trench and is thus on the way to ultimate consumption in 3 or 4 million years' time.

The Cocos (Keeling) Islands were the only coral atolls that Charles Darwin visited in 1836, when he developed his well-known theory of atoll formation. He considered that the up-growth of coral reefs continued long after the seamounts that supported them had subsided. The thickness of the corals underlying Cocos is not known, but the dredging of basaltic rocks in local waters suggests that it is in the order of 500–1000m.

Coral reefs are composed of myriads of coral polyps, together with calcareous algae

7

and numerous other shelly organisms which have two major requirements for growth and survival. The water in which the corals live must be between 20° C and 30° C, and the algae that live with them need sunlight for photosynthesis. Coral reefs can therefore develop only in the surface layers of tropical seas down to a maximum depth of 50–80 m.

Coral material has been found at depths of over 1000 m beneath atolls in the Pacific Ocean. Glacial sea-level changes alone cannot account for this depth of growth, so it must be assumed that these reefs were also built upon sinking foundations. Seafloor subsidence is known to occur as new crustal material spreads further from its origin at the mid-oceanic ridges. As it moves it gradually becomes cooler, thicker and denser. Darwin had not yet heard of plate tectonics, but his basic ideas on atoll formation are still accepted today.

A living reef creates a narrow fringing platform around a landmass. The corals develop just below the surface of the water and produce an area of shoals and shallows that can be hazardous for seafarers. Where shingle and rubble is piled up by storms and heavy seas, a small, flat islet can begin to form and build up with white sand from the eroding fragments of coral and other marine skeletons.

In the sheltered areas behind the outer, fringing reef there may be boulders of coral material that have been torn off its edges during storms and later deposited in calmer water. In the quiet waters away from the surf this coral may grow into remarkable mushroom and pinnacle shapes and support a whole community of marine life. The water in a coral-fringed lagoon is shallow, although not as shallow as over the reef itself. The lagoon floor is covered by the sandy sediments of broken coral and the remains of millions of marine creatures.

The seaward edge of a coral reef is largely composed of the skeletons of the calcite-excreting algae, as these calcareous remnants are better than corals at withstanding the impact of the thundering surf. The outermost slope of the reef is usually littered with fragments that have broken off from the more exposed upper sections.

GEOMORPHOLOGY

Once a sandy atoll has been formed, its surface features are sculpted by the ravages of wind and wave action. Weathering, erosion, transportation and deposition of coral debris occur under the influence of tides, currents, climate and human activities.

There have been a number of changes on the southern Cocos atoll since Darwin's visit last century. Sand and mud, derived from the remains of the marine animals of the reef, have further accumulated inside the lagoon. In the early days of settlement, access to South Island was relatively easy. Later it became

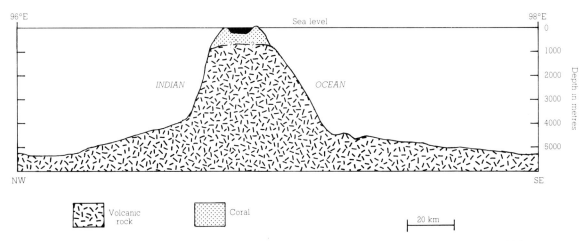

A north-west to south-east cross-section of the Cocos (Keeling) Islands (*after Jacobson, 1976*)

necessary to dredge boating channels and now the island is only accessible to shallow-draughted vessels at high tide.

The shapes of the islands are continually changing under the dual influences of erosion and deposition. During his visit, Charles Darwin was shown an old chart that suggested South Island had once been a series of separate islands. Evidence of the channels between these old islands is quite obvious today in the nature of South Island's soil and vegetation. The ebb and flow of water through these old passages between the islands has left clearly visible drainage patterns in the banks of sea grasses on the southern lagoon floor.

Some of the narrow channels between the smaller islets in Darwin's time later became clogged with volcanic debris from Krakatoa's 1883 eruption. North Keeling has a broad pumice beach on its eastern shore and heavy storms today can still expose pumice boulders as large as soccer balls beneath the sands of most of the islands.

The ocean perimeters of the two Cocos atolls are subjected to the continual attack of ocean swells which originate in the Roaring Forties (40° S latitude) and the south-east tradewind belt of the Indian Ocean. The fringing reef dissipates most of the swells' energy, however, and only relatively small waves can reach the shore. These waves carry coral sand and fragments inshore, along the beaches and into the lagoon.

North Keeling Island is believed to have once been a series of smaller islets. It is now a single island with a central lagoon that opens to the windward side. The lagoon itself is very shallow and sandy-bottomed and does not contain any living coral. Instead there are large patches of sea-grass, broken fragments of which accumulate on the windy lagoon shores. The build-up of bird droppings in the soil of this atoll indicates a very early stage in the development of the phosphate deposits that characterise Christmas Island. It would appear that the North Keeling lagoon is slowly filling with sediment and that its shores are

Seaward edge of the
reef platform

gradually becoming colonised by vegetation. A long sand-spit extending to the north-west of the island points to the direction of its possible future growth.

The horseshoe shapes and curves of many of the Cocos islands illustrate the way in which sandy coral cays tend to grow at their extremities, curve in on themselves and eventually encircle their own lagoons. Horsburgh Island, at the northern end of the southern atoll, has completed this cycle and has only a small brackish lake to remind us of its earlier lagoon. Many of the tiny islands between Home and South Island display similar tendencies as they slowly encroach upon their own lagoonlets.

GROUNDWATER

The larger islands of the Cocos atoll are comprised of coral sands overlying a hardpan layer of coral breccia, which corresponds to the 'barrier' or reef-flat. Beneath the metre-thick hard layer is a zone of coarse, saturated coral sand. This sand acts as an aquifer and may contain a 'lens' of fresh water floating above saltier water. Rainwater permeates down into this saturated layer and eventually flows back into the surrounding sea through a transition zone of brackish water.

The minimum width of a coral island necessary to generate a permanent supply of fresh water is estimated to be 400 m. This means that there is no substantial underground water supply on most of the atoll's smaller islands, nor on Direction Island. Wells dug on the thin ring of land that comprises North Keeling have produced only brackish water. This island is also too narrow to develop a freshwater lens. West Island has three separate areas with substantial reserves of fresh water. The thickness of these and other lenses fluctuates daily with the rise and fall of the tides, the incidence of rainfall and the patterns of human consumption.

CLIMATE

The Cocos (Keeling) Islands lie in the path of the south-east tradewinds for most of the year. Weather patterns are extremely uniform, with the prevailing winds from the south-east about 85 per cent of the time.

The islands are situated in a cyclone-prone region and are often affected by passing cyclonic systems during the summer months. The cyclone that is able to pinpoint and sweep right over Cocos is infrequent, however, and these seem to arise only three or four times a century. In recent times, Cyclone Doreen passed overhead and caused widespread destruction in January 1968 and an immature Cyclone Frederic brought minor damage in January 1988.

Cyclonic winds of up to 180 km per hour have been recorded in the Territory, as have very large ocean swells and occasional storm surges. More common are windy squalls, with gusts of up to 70 km per hour, that bring heavy showers as they pass over the islands at almost any time of the year. The south-east trade-winds are most persistent from June to September and strongest in August. This is also the coolest time of the year when maxima average around 27° C and minima around 23° C. The annual range of temperatures in the territory rarely exceeds 8° C.

Rainfall is relatively heavy from April to June and drops off markedly by August, reaching the low for the year during September–November. Average annual rainfall is in the order of 2000 mm (see Appendix).

October and November are transitional months as the doldrum season settles in for the summer. December to April marks the cyclone season as the Intertropical Front (ITF) moves as far south as Cocos. On several occasions, most recently in March 1983, the ITF has moved so far south as to permit a period of dominant north-westerly winds. This El Niño-related pattern can have a detrimental effect on lagoon ecology as the corals and algae depend on the south-easterly airstream to continually flush new seawater through the lagoon.

Storm-generated waves
crash on the reef edge

TIDES AND CURRENTS

Tides experienced in the Territory are semi-diurnal, with two high and two low tides daily. The change from one extreme to the other takes roughly six hours and the turn of the tide needs about half an hour to travel from the north of the lagoon to the south. The overall range of tides in the territory is about 1.2 m. This varies from a maximum of 1.4 m above datum for the highest tides down to 0.2 m for the lowest. At low tide, beaches approximately 20–50 m wide are exposed around the outside of the islands.

In general terms, the local currents flow in a northerly direction, both inside and outside the lagoon. This movement is driven by the south-east tradewinds and the convergence of the northward-flowing West Australian coastal current and the westward-flowing equatorial drift.

VEGETATION

Today the principal vegetation of the Cocos (Keeling) Islands is row upon row of coconut palms (*Cocos nucifera*), reflecting the atoll's recent history as a copra plantation. Little is known of the structure and composition of the original vegetation of the islands; however North Keeling Island, while also modified, is believed to be fairly representative of the original flora. Certainly, coconut palms must have been widely represented before human settlement for the islands to have been named 'Cocos'.

One species of tree, the locally-named Iron-wood (*Cordia subcordata*), apparently once formed extensive stands of forest on several islands but has now been reduced to small clumps of stunted trees as a consequence of its value for house and boat construction. Remaining trees have been heavily lopped to provide firewood and raw material for carvings. The shores of the small brackish swamp on Horsburgh Island are littered with the stumps of large Ironwoods that once formed part of an extensive forest on the island. Similar relics are also found on the lagoon shores of South Island.

The vegetation on the southern atoll today consists largely of coconut palms in plantations of varying ages and heights, beneath which there may be an extensive shrub layer or a sparse carpet of coarse grasses or other perennials. The shrubs often form dense thickets up to a metre in height on the seaward fringes of each island, but where the coconut canopy closes over, in semi-mature plantations, there is often no living ground cover, only a dense mat of decaying palm fronds. Other types of leaf litter are scarcely seen as they are quickly disposed of by the vast numbers of Land Crabs (*Cardisoma carnifex*) which abound on most of the islands.

Along the lagoon shores, particularly in the southern regions, a gnarled, stunted shrub (*Pemphis acidula*) occupies the 'new land': the sandy spits, bars and reclaimed lagoonlets.

The seaward sides of the coconut groves are typically flanked by a thick growth of Cabbage Bush (*Scaevola sericea*) and a few stunted, thick-barked trees (*Argusia argentea*). Clumps of Pandanus (*Pandanus tectorius*) can be found on the eastward-facing shores of the lagoon and the windswept ocean sides of the eastern islands.

SOIL

The land surface is covered to a depth of between 10 cm and one metre with a calcareous sand mixed with coral shingle. On areas covered by vegetation, this sandy soil is supplemented with a small amount of decaying organic matter. The coral sand and shingle mixture forms the main parent material for soil development on the atoll.

Blocks of pumice from the eruptions of Tomboro (1815) and Krakatoa (1883) are scattered widely but have not had time to play a major role in soil formation. Neither have the areas of stony ballast and clay bricks left in various places by visiting vessels during World War II. Those areas that have been littered with husked coconuts, slashed undergrowth or seaweed deposits display a more distinctive soil profile. They possess the thinnest of dark topsoils overlying the grey-coloured calcareous

sands. Generally speaking, soils on the atoll are alkaline, quite thin and deficient in a number of nutrients.

Soils have been imported from such places as Christmas Island and Singapore, and possibly from Mauritius and Java, to provide an improved growing medium for introduced fruit trees, vegetables and other plants of economic importance. These imported soils have been used on Horsburgh, Direction, Home and South Islands.

Cocos nucifera dominates the southern atoll

13

The Living World 2

2

The ocean throwing its waters over the broad reef appears an invincible, all-powerful enemy: yet we see it resisted, and even conquered, by means which at first seem most weak and inefficient.

Charles Darwin, describing the Cocos reef in 1836.

The contrast between the above-water and the below-water worlds on remote coral atolls is immense. Apart from seabirds, limited vegetation and man there is not a great deal to hold our attention in the above-water living environment. Beneath the waves it is an entirely different story.

The ecosystem of a coral reef is not unlike that of a rainforest in that it contains an enormous range of species. There is also a vertical zonation of habitats and a highly complex food web. The chains and networks of interrelationships between organisms on a coral reef are so involved that they have defied even computer-based efforts to list every one of the links.

THE CORAL REEF

Corals are tiny animals no more than a centimetre in size. They are related to sea anemones and jellyfish in the family of animals known as the *Coelenterates*. Like the anemone, a single coral animal is a polyp. It has one or more rings of tentacles surrounding a mouth that leads to a central cavity in a stalk that is able to contract. On the tentacles are small stinging darts with which it captures passing plankton.

In most types of coral any polyp can reproduce by budding off new individuals from its body. Colonies of millions of polyps are created in this way, with each organism connected to its neighbours by living tissue.

Corals are extraordinary animals. The polyps and the tissues that connect them have the ability to secrete a limestone skeleton. One polyp may be unspectacular but coral colonies can produce large boulders, table tops,

tree branches and all manner of other exquisite and complex shapes. World-wide there are over a thousand different species of coral and each has its own way of depositing the limestone it creates. Any one species is capable of producing a wide variety of shapes in the differing zones of the same atoll. The end result of all this budding, secreting and outgrowth is a coral reef.

When one considers the depth of coral material beneath islands like Cocos, it is hard not to be overcome by the sheer scale of this most spectacular natural phenomenon.

Reefs tend to grow by spreading outwards more than upwards and consequently they produce a flat platform with a steep outer edge. On the Cocos (Keeling) Islands this fringing reef-flat varies from 100–400 m in width around the outside of the southern atoll. Living corals are sparse in this zone, as there is usually little or even no water at low tide. Towards the outer edge of the reef-flat the platform takes on a higher elevation and breaks into a series of spurs and grooves which act as a surge system. This is the zone that takes the brunt of wave-attack. The reef barrier itself is a deceptively dangerous place in which to bathe or swim. After a series of waves have filled the area with water, a returning rip current will drain away the surplus. These rips occur every few hundred metres along the barrier and have claimed a number of lives over the years.

Beyond its visible edge, the reef slopes down gradually into a zone of active outward growth. On the western side of the atoll this outer slope is sandy in parts and it varies in width from 10–100 m. It is far narrower on the windswept eastern and southern fringes of the atoll. This part of the reef abounds in all manner of beautiful and delicate corals. Just beyond them the gradual slope of the outer reef ends abruptly in the spectacular, almost perpendicular, 'drop-off' that never ceases to fascinate all those who dive around coral atolls.

Strictly speaking, the term 'coral reef' is a misnomer. Certainly the corals produce a vast amount of the rocky material, but without the plants of the reef there would be no reef at all. Plants are the basis of life on a coral reef just as they are in all other ecosystems. They fix the sun's energy into a useable chemical form and they are also vital in the limestone depositing process.

Where are all these plants? Most of them are single-celled and living inside the tissues of the hard and soft corals. Others, equally microscopic, clump together and build up the stony ramparts that absorb the bulk of the fury of the ocean. These calcareous red algae are able to lay down rock, just as corals do, but right in the turbulent surf zone.

The algal cells within the coral tissue share a symbiotic relationship with the corals that harbour them. Some corals contain over one million algal cells for every square centimetre of coral surface. Other corals have none.

Both the algae and the hosting corals gain from their relationship. The algae take up the waste products of the polyp and use them for their own metabolism. The carbon dioxide from the coral's respiration is used by the algae in photosynthesis. The oxygen and carbohydrate produced by the algae are both required by the polyp. There is a close recycling of other biochemicals as well, so very little overall waste occurs. Corals that have this relationship with algae are able to produce greater quantities of limestone than corals without them.

Most of a reef's plant life is algal. Seaweeds are present, but are not immediately obvious on a coral reef as they are constantly being eaten back by the flocks of grazing herbivores. These grazers include parrot fish, sea urchins and a wide variety of shellfish.

The coral reef has a greater variety of life upon it and within it than any other oceanic ecosystem. The food chains are by no means simple. The reef's carnivores eat a wide variety of other life forms. The predatory cone-shell, for example, may eat other molluscs (herbivores), crustaceans (carnivores) or worms (debris feeders). Anything which eats a coral consumes both the animal and its captive plant cells. Corals themselves feed on the planktonic larvae of every species as well as depending on their own internal algaes.

Sea urchins are one of the most obvious herbivores on the reef. They can always be seen in the clear water of the barrier. They have relatively few natural enemies because their sharp outer spines contain light sensors that keep these weapons constantly pointed upwards while the animal grazes in security below them.

Some fish are herbivores. These include the well-known parrot and surgeon fish families. Their beak-like mouths are adapted to rasping algae off the coral rock, making a constant clicking sound that is audible to a diver. Schools of these blunt, solid fish move through the coral gardens like cows in pasture. In their throats they possess further sets of teeth that powder the limestone so that they can utilise the algae and live polyps within it. The useless grit is then ejected. Over thousands of years this coral grit has helped to amass beds of fine, white sand on the lagoon floor.

Many of the brightly coloured butterfly fish are coral feeders and have long, retractable snouts that reach inside the coral skeleton to extract the polyps.

Moorish Idols (*Zanclus cornutus*) swim in a coral garden

Starfish, cones, octopuses, eels, sharks and barracuda are the main predators of the reef. They are constantly on the hunt. Their continual presence has led to the development of a wide range of defence mechanisms by their prey. Many of the coral-grinding fish, for example, have a slimy outer coating. This is secreted at night in their rocky crevasse homes to ward off the unwanted attention of moray eels. Other animals are armed, some are camouflaged, some seek the protection of other species, some use mimicry, bright colours and various defensive behaviours. All will jealously guard their rocky shelters in the labyrinthine mass of coral rock.

As mentioned above, the coral reef ecosystem displays a number of parallels with a tropical rainforest. Here, as in jungle, a great many small creatures act as rubbish collectors and recyclers. The crabs and snail species are scavengers. They rapidly locate and dispose of any rotting flesh or wasted food. Others are debris feeders: animals like worms and sea cucumbers, that consume the coral sand, extract nutrients from it and expel it once more. Most prolific of all, yet invisible to the observer, are the microscopic bacteria that coat rock surfaces, crevasses and any decaying matter. Just like the jungle, the reef depends on a rapid and efficient recycling of nutrients and organic matter. The rubbish collectors of the coral reef perform their task so well that little is lost to the wider ocean.

THE LAGOON

Coral reefs have a certain uniformity of profile, wherever they might be found. The reef-flat has both an inner and an outer edge. The inside edge slopes gently and gradually flattens out into a coral lagoon. The floor of a lagoon is typically a sandy plain with countless mounds of coral rock, known in Australian waters as 'bommies'. These may be covered with corals and teeming with fish — in direct contrast to the barren, sandy plains around them.

The southern Cocos lagoon is strewn with these coral lumps, but is also characterised by a large number of deep 'blue holes' in its mid-section. These vary in width and depth and the water in them is usually clouded with sediment. The sides of these holes are covered with a dead, broken forest of staghorn coral and their bases are characterised by loose, slowly settling silt. While it is obvious that the lagoon is silting up at a rapid rate, it also appears to have suffered a greater ecological tragedy.

The southern Cocos lagoon was badly affected by the widely destructive El Niño-related events of March 1983. Documentation exists of similar ecological disturbances in 1876 and 1961. Local Malay residents can readily recall other times when a phenomenon they call *air busuk* (smelly water) has occurred in their lagoon. It would seem that these events have occurred at least three times in the last 30 years, with a number of minor episodes in between.

Southern lagoon shore

MARCH 1983 — AN ECOLOGICAL TRAGEDY

In early 1983 the entire Southern Hemisphere was affected by a generalised climatic disturbance. Severe drought was experienced in South Africa, Australia and Indonesia. Record flooding rains descended on Ecuador and the anchovy fisheries of Peru failed dismally.

The mechanism involved is quite complex, but it relates to large-scale fluctuations in atmospheric pressure. The amplitude of these fluctuations in 1983 was particularly high and coincided with a more southerly than usual transit of the Intertropical Front (ITF). Around the Cocos (Keeling) Islands the combined effect produced alternate north-westerly winds and prolonged calms. Temperatures were unusually high and there was a lot of thunderstorm activity.

This contrasted markedly with the usual alternate pattern of south-easterlies and calms at this time of year. The regular south-east tradewinds are vital for seawater flushing of the lagoon. Ocean water usually pours into the lagoon from the major openings in the southern and eastern rims of the atoll and this promotes a general flow of water from south to north.

During March 1983 the foul smell of rotten eggs began to emanate from the lagoon and an area of discoloured water appeared to the south and west of Home Island. This gradually extended across the lagoon towards the West Island jetty. Dead fish began to float to the surface and others schooled around as though drunk. They were joined by dozens of normally well-hidden moray eels. Great masses of fish milled around aimlessly in the shallows.

They were all territorial, bottom-dwelling fish. There was not a shark or other pelagic fish in sight; they had vanished from the lagoon. After a day or two countless thousands of dead fish floated on the water and were being washed up, bloated and putrid, onto the shores of Home Island, Direction Island and West Island. This situation continued for a week as the area of foul water grew in size to cover about one-third of the lagoon.

Without the natural flushing mechanism the ebbing tides drew the polluted water out of the lagoon's eastern openings and even discoloured the surrounding sea. The foul water remained in the lagoon for another week before the south-east tradewinds resumed in earnest and flushed it out.

This phenomenon is known as eutrophication. Due to the marked reduction in the lagoon's nutrient and oxygen levels, a massive breakdown occurred in the millions of algal cells within the lagoon's corals. Algae in this state produce a highly toxic, acidic substance that is capable of killing most marine life with which it comes into contact.

Life in the Cocos-Keeling lagoon is obviously very precarious. The periodic occurence of eutrophication, together with the intense solar heating of the increasingly shallow water, reduced salinity at times of heavy rains and massive silting all contribute to the paucity of life in the southern Cocos lagoon.

A white Ghost Crab
(*Ocypode ceratophthalma*)
excavating in the
intertidal zone

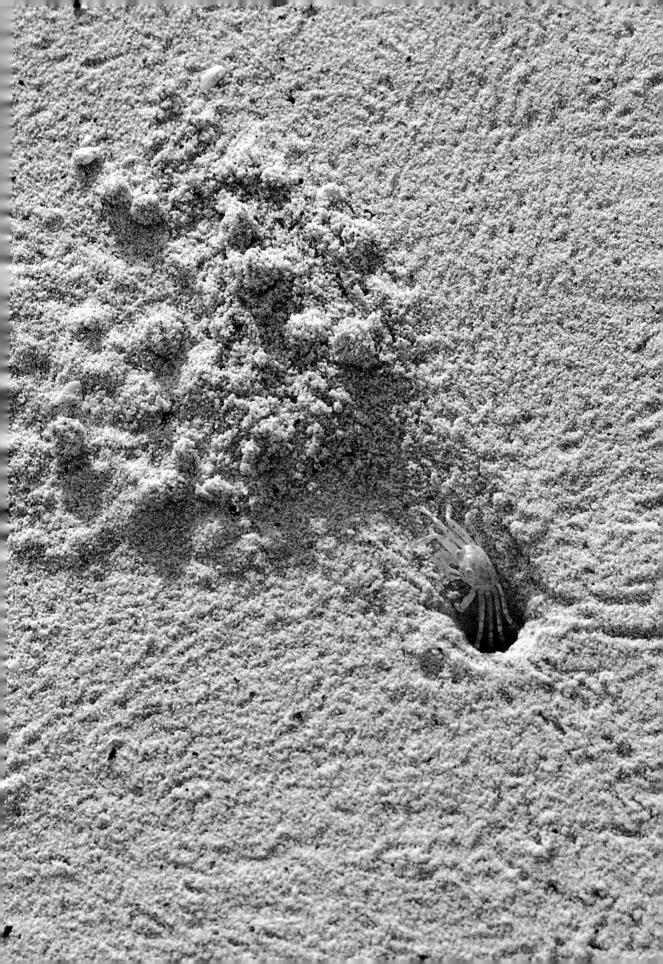

Orange-green variety
of Ghost Crab
(*Ocypode ceratophthalma*)

THE SHORELINE

In striking contrast to the world beneath the waves, the shoreline of an atoll contains the least diversity of life to be found anywhere on a coral island. The shore marks the boundary between the land and the sea. It may be rocky or sandy and it may span a number of different habitats — from the wave-washed tidal zone to higher areas affected mainly by ocean spray.

Any organisms that choose the shoreline for their home must adapt to its special problems. They must be able to withstand the surge of the waves, the midday sun, high levels of salt, wind and wave erosion, limited food supply, the tidal ebb and flow and the occasional buffeting storm. Animals that live along the shoreline are generally small and well-armoured. The breaking waves bring them food, but also threaten to wash them out to sea. Those that live above the tidal reaches run the risk of drying out. The lives of animals along the shoreline are therefore characterised by a constant feast-or-famine seesaw.

Plants in this zone are the hardy pioneers of island vegetation. They are salt-tolerant, drought-resistant and well adapted to constant wind. The very sand in which they grow is liable to shift and erode. Despite these harsh conditions, their annual patterns of seed dispersal, growth and development persist. These plants are the islands' main defence against erosion.

Cocos shores display a number of moods. During the summer doldrum season some may present the 'classic' image of mirror-calm seas, sparkling sand and gently rustling palm leaves. Not all are blessed with a sandy beach, however, and very few have sand-flats that extend far enough to permit swimming. There are often days with a full cloud cover and others again with howling gales and wind-whipped waves. Typically, a spray-laden south-easterly wind sweeps across the islands. Shorelines that face straight into these trade-winds present living things with a far tougher habitat than those on the islands' leeward sides.

Shoreline plants provide a protective ring around each island and are living examples of the way in which pioneer plants colonise remote coral cays. Those nearest to the water are the low-profile, salt-tolerant, wind-resistant species of ground covers, grasses and herbs. Further from the water, along the inland edge of the beach, is a zone of hardy shrubs and low trees. Here one finds the gnarled Octopus Bush (*Argusia argentea*), the moisture-storing Cabbage Bush (*Scaevola sericea*) and a few stands of the stilt-like Pandanus Palm (*Pandanus tectorius*).

The brackish, now-enclosed inlet on Horsburgh Island is the only place in the territory that supports a community of mangroves (*Rhizophora stylosa*). These trees have the unique ability to tolerate high levels of salt and low levels of oxygen around their roots. Unlike the stabilising shrubs of the beach margins, they can grow at a level where their roots are continually immersed in salt water. This warm, shallow, salty swamp is fed by percolating sea-water at high tide.

One type of animal dominates the shoreline. This is the domain of crabs. Many of these creatures appear equally content on either side of the water's edge while others are more obviously land dwellers. However, all reflect their species' ancient marine origins in their dependence on the sea during their breeding cycles.

Shoreline creatures are scavengers. The action of waves, reduced somewhat by the reef-flat, constantly brings in organic debris. This is dumped along the water's edge and forms a broken line along the high tide mark. Crabs make good use of whatever nutrients they can find among it. Added to this marine debris are quantities of plant material from the shrubs and trees of the strand line.

Crabs compete with each other for the available food. Some are fast-moving daytime scavengers, others are more nocturnal. The rows of holes and sandpiles along the inter-tidal slopes belong to the Ghost Crabs (*Ocypode ceratophthalma*). They shelter by day in these moist burrows and emerge around sunset to conduct a hurried routine of feeding and digging. These crabs, with their eyes on stalks, often seek refuge in the foamy edge of the sea. Their periscope eyes then keep a sharp lookout for predatory shore-birds.

Shoreline life is similar to desert life in that most of its creatures are nocturnal and able to live beneath the hot surface of the sand during the day. Bacteria, worms, sand-fleas and crabs all make their homes in the cooler, moist layers below the surface. Their predators, mostly birds and other crabs, display a range of adaptations that enable them to hunt the bur-rowers. Shoreline birds generally have long, spindly legs, an elongated neck and a sharp, pointed beak. This gives them the necessary height, reach and piercing ability to scavenge along the water's edge. Several species of heron can be seen patrolling the Cocos shore-line at any time of day. The crabs themselves display fearsome claws that permit them to crack open and tear up any larger food items that may come their way — including other crabs.

After the Ghost Crab, with its tell-tale holes and sand piles, the next most conspicuous beach dweller is the Hermit Crab (*Coenobita perlata*). The major problem faced by these creatures is the fact that their large abdomens are soft and vulnerable. They must protect themselves by backing into and hanging on to an empty mollusc shell. In time, as each crab outgrows its home, it seeks another to replace it. There is never a shortage of empty mollusc shells along the Cocos beaches.

The largest of all the shoreline creatures is the occasional visiting turtle. Only a few come ashore on the southern Cocos atoll, as entry is rather difficult and fraught with the risk of capture by humans. Tell-tale flippered trails can sometimes be seen on the sands near the rifle range and the north point of West Island. Here there are breaks in the reef that permit relatively easy access to the shore. Another opening occurs at Alor Penyu on West Island. The name of this sandy bay actually means 'turtle passage' in Malay; however, no turtles

have been recorded here in recent times. These days they seem to prefer the more remote and steeply shelving western beach of North Keeling Island.

The two main varieties of this creature to be seen in Cocos waters are the large Green Turtle (*Chelonia mydas*) and the smaller Hawksbill (*Eretmochelys imbricata*). The former is largely a vegetarian, living on a var-iety of marine plants and seagrasses and the latter is a carnivore. The Hawksbill is so-named because of its beak-like upper jaw. It lives on jellyfish and other soft-bodied marine creatures.

Large numbers of turtles were once kept penned in an enclosed tidal pond on the lagoon-side of Home Island. Unfortunately the islands' centenary celebrations in 1927 put paid to almost the entire herd. Only a few large turtles are sighted in Cocos waters today.

The lagoon-side shores of the atoll slope extremely gently down to the water's edge. There are many muddy tidal flats. Most of these shorelines are characterised by a build-up of seaweeds and other floating debris. The lagoon shore of West Island is the final resting place of hundreds of palm logs, ripped from other islands during cyclones. These shores provide a banquet of vegetable matter for the ubiquitous Land Crabs (*Cardisoma car-nifex*). The upper reaches of the tidal flats are populated by millions of tiny Fiddler Crabs (*Uca gaimardi*) and the deeper flats by the occasional large Mud Crab (*Thalamita spinimana*) and solidly built House Crabs (*Calappa hepatica*).

THE FOREST

The lonely island of North Keeling is the only place on the Cocos (Keeling) Islands that can boast a natural forest. All the other islands in the group have been steadily transformed into coconut groves. The western arm of North Keeling is covered by a Pisonia and Coconut forest. *Pisonia grandis* is a medium-sized,

Land Crab (*Cardisoma carnifex*)

Green Turtle (*Chelonia mydas*) (*Courtesy Coo-ee Picture Library*)

large-leafed tree common to many tropical islands. It reaches a height of 15–20 m, has an uneven spreading crown, yellowish-green leaves, smooth grey bark and broad-buttressed roots. Its timber is rather soft and its branches break easily. Beneath the leafy canopy the forest air is hot and still and the light takes on a greenish hue. Here and there the forest floor is stabbed by a shaft of bright sunlight. There is no real undergrowth, but the ground is strewn with coconuts and these grow rapidly whenever the canopy cover is broken.

Coconuts line the seaward margins of the forest, together with the typical shoreline shrubs and stunted Argusia trees. The lagoon shores of the forest are protected by a thick band of wind-sculpted Argusia, palms and clumps of the gnarly Ironwood.

The Pisonia belt is the domain of the Red-Footed Booby Bird (*Sula sula*). These rather raucous birds like to build their rough nests in the forest canopy and make their presence felt by their continual squawking and flapping overhead. In direct contrast, the tiny, modest White Terns (*Gygis alba*) lay their single, speckled eggs directly onto the low, rough-barked branches of the Argusia trees. They silently guard and incubate their solitary egg by covering it with their delicate stomach feathers. The dimly lit floor of the forest is the home of the elusive Cocos Buff-Banded Rail (*Rallus philippensis andrewsi*). These fast-running scavengers build their nests in the dark recesses of fallen logs, tree stumps or the spreading roots of a Pisonia tree. They are the only endemic subspecies of bird to be found in the Territory.

Opposite:
North Keeling Forest

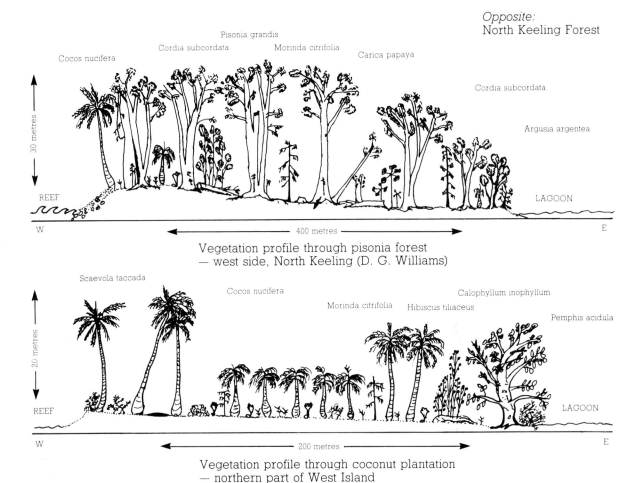

Vegetation profile through pisonia forest
— west side, North Keeling (D. G. Williams)

Vegetation profile through coconut plantation
— northern part of West Island
(D. G. Williams)

Even more elusive an inhabitant of the forest floor is the giant Robber Crab (*Birgus latro*). These blue and orange crustaceans can grow to quite large and powerful proportions. Their long pincers exert a remarkable force and they are expert climbers. Largely nocturnal, these creatures were eagerly sought by the Cocos Malay people as food. Their local name of *udang darat*, meaning land crayfish, sums up their unusual appearance quite accurately. Nowadays, very few are ever spotted on the islands of the southern atoll. Another Keeling crab that is rarely seen elsewhere on Cocos is the shiny Red and Black Crab (*Gecaroidea humei natalis*), although its numbers are quite small and in nowhere near the seasonal 'plague proportions' that are seen on Christmas Island.

The southern sweep of North Keeling is clothed in a thick *Pemphis acidula* scrub. This area is battered constantly by salty spray and is the windy breeding ground of several species of Terns, Frigate Birds, Masked and Brown Boobies and the occasional Red-Tailed Tropic Bird. Human access to this area is carefully controlled by the Australian National Parks and Wildlife Service, as the breeding birds are inclined to take to the air and neglect their eggs when disturbed. The Pemphis shrub is an evergreen with a short and twisted trunk. Here it mainly occurs in patches with bare or grassy areas in between. It is set fairly well back from the shoreline, behind an area of salt-resistant grasses and ground-hugging herbs.

The northern and north-eastern reaches of the Keeling atoll display the greatest variety of plant species. This is probably due to the prevailing wind pattern which makes this area the final resting place for all manner of wind-blown and sea-borne seeds. The exact origin of an extensive area of *Cocos nucifera* in the north-east of the island is a puzzle, however. These palms may have been planted, although the area lacks the classic grid pattern of a plantation. They could also have developed naturally following the destruction of a section of Pisonia forest during a severe storm.

THE SKIES

The island of North Keeling has a world-wide reputation as a seabird rookery, whereas the main atoll, only 24 km to the south, is almost devoid of birdlife. This amazing contrast

A large Robber Crab
(*Birgus latro*)

between the two atolls is a stark reminder of the powerful influence that humans can have upon natural island ecosystems.

As nineteenth century commercial interests extended into the Indian and Pacific Oceans, coral islands gradually became transformed into production sites for foreign markets. The effects of this enterprise were unfortunately not limited to the mere replacement of plant species. Along with every stand of hardwood that was demolished, went the homes of many animals and smaller plants. Most noticeable of these were the birds which nested in the trees. The natural diversity of tropical islands was drastically reduced when they were cleared for plantations. Typically, the plantation workers' food rations were sufficiently miserly to force them to further deplete each island's

Sooty Terns (*Sterna fuscata*) and Common Noddies (*Anous stolidus*) fill the air on a windy North Keeling beach

Masked Booby (*Sula dactylatra*),
North Keeling

resources in order to supplement their
meagre diet. In this way birds and birds' eggs,
turtles and turtle eggs, shellfish and coconut
crabs by the thousand were taken as necessary food supplements on many tropical island
plantations.

Commercial Man's influence did not stop
there. He took with him his familiar ornamen-
tal and food-bearing European plants as well

as a menagerie of alien animals. On the
southern Cocos atoll the combined effect of the
predations of Man, rats and cats has been to
create a silent, sterile coconut monoculture
which itself now suffers from neglect. The
sighting of birds in the skies overhead is an
event that draws comment from all who witness it. Somehow, North Keeling Island has
managed to escape this total transformation by

virtue of its splendid isolation and difficulty of access. It is truly another world.

The skies above North Keeling are filled with thousands of wheeling seabirds. Any walk along this island's southern beaches has one ducking for cover from the attention of terns and choosing one's footsteps carefully around the ground-nesting boobies.

The most common bird on North Keeling is the Red-Footed Booby (*Sula sula*). It feeds on flying fish, squid and small surface fish. It nests in trees and shrubs and usually lays a single egg each year. It is a very inquisitive species and this, together with its size, has led to its being a popular target for bird hunters. Another common bird on North Keeling is the Frigate Bird of both the Least and Great varieties (*Fregata ariel*, *Fregata minor*). They too are expert fishermen, although they will often opt for the easier exercise of stealing a Booby's catch.

Masked and Brown Boobies (*Sula dactylatra*, *Sula leucogaster*) can be found in smaller numbers on the exposed southern foreshores of the island, as can the elusive Red-Tailed Tropic Bird (*Phaethon rubricauda*). These windy, rocky shores also attract Sooty Terns (*Sterna fuscata*), Common Noddies (*Anous stolidus*) and the delicate, fairy-like White Tern (*Gygis alba*).

The bleached white stumps of Ironwood trees that litter the saltmarsh in the northwestern corner of North Keeling provide hollows for the occasional nests of White-Tailed Tropic Birds (*Phaethon lepturus*). These birds can gracefully skim very low over the ocean, using their long tail feathers as stabilisers while they pluck small fish from the surface waters.

Nowadays, the Australian National Parks and Wildlife Service carefully monitors bird numbers and the Cocos (Keeling) Islands Council has agreed to a seabird management plan for the territory. The collection of birds for food is now sufficiently restricted to permit their continued existence on the northern atoll. It is rather ironical to recall that the very abundance of seabirds probably influenced the early settlers in their choice of these islands as a place to settle.

A tiny White Tern
(*Gygis alba*)
guards its single egg,
North Keeling

PLANT AND ANIMAL COLONISATION OF COCOS

These wind-swept sandy cays that emerged from the Indian Ocean some 30 million years ago have long been covered with vegetation and populated by small animals. On several occasions, huge storm waves may have swept the atoll bare again and the agents of colonisation would have had to begin afresh. Only the most hardy species could have survived in such a forbidding environment.

The first successful colonists were those whose normal habitat is the windy, exposed shoreline. The seeds of shoreline plants are well adapted for dispersal by ocean currents and can survive well in low-nutrient, salty conditions. Pandanus Palms and the stunted Octopus Bush have seeds that are surrounded by a cork-like layer and can remain alive in seawater for up to six months. Only when washed ashore and soaked by rainwater will they begin to germinate.

Hardy bushes and succulent ground-covering plants have gradually modified the stark, original habitat. They have contributed organic matter from their own wastes and dead remains, held moisture, trapped and stabilised soil as well as modifying the light, temperature and wind exposure conditions on the surface of the sandy cays. These plants would also have provided a limited source of food for any creatures that may have chanced upon the islands. Seabirds, finding a convenient and safe resting place, may have helped to introduce other plant species. The seed of the Pisonia tree is especially sticky and easily transported by migratory birds. No doubt these birds also contributed further nutrients to the embryonic soil from their bodily wastes and decaying remains.

The best-known of the ocean-borne seeds of the tropics are the large nuts of the coconut palm. These will take root on new islets that have managed to build up sufficient sand above high water.

Ocean currents are also involved in the dispersal of terrestrial species with marine stages in their life cycles. The larvae of shore-line crabs are circulated far and wide by the movements of the sea. As long as they find sufficient plant material to eat, crabs will be among the earliest island colonisers. Their burrowing behaviour then enhances the development of a simple soil which, in turn, will aid the establishment of new plant species.

Fungi, lichens, mosses and many microscopic animals have spores that are so tiny that they can be carried long distances by wind. Prevailing winds and high-altitude jet streams may transport them hundreds or even thousands of kilometres. The tiny spores can act as condensation nuclei for raindrops and fall to earth over oceanic islands. It is sometimes possible for larger organisms such as spiders, insects and birds to be blown vast distances by storms or cyclones.

The most obvious wind-blown insects are the groups of large dragonflies that appear from time to time. These creatures require fresh water in which to breed and rarely reproduce locally. Their arrival is usually preceded by a few days of strong easterly or north-easterly winds that are followed by a calm. Several stray bats, owls, waders and swallows have been recorded on the islands in recent years. They, too, could only have been blown here.

Wind-blown immigrants may carry a cargo of other potential colonists, both externally and internally. These might include seeds, bacteria and parasitic insects.

Top right:
Brown Booby
(*Sula dactylatra*),
North Keeling

Bottom right:
Red-footed Booby
(*Sula sula*),
North Keeling

The patterns of wind and current circulation are important in determining the potential immigrant species for an island, but so too are the freakish quirks of wind and weather. A single, solitary seal has even found its way to Horsburgh Island, to the great surprise of the Malay workers who spotted it. A local legend tells of a 'mermaid' on Prison Island. She, too, may have been a stray seal or a dugong. Generally speaking, the further an island is from a large landmass the fewer the number of species that are present. The specialised adaptations necessary for survival at sea selectively eliminate many potential colonists.

Enormous sawn logs of tropical hardwoods are a common form of flotsam on Cocos beaches today. So too are craypot marker buoys from Fremantle and Geraldton in Western Australia. An outrigger canoe and an inflatable boat from a holiday resort have been washed ashore in recent times, as have metres and metres of sheet rubber used in the making of rubber thongs. The majority of this modern-day flotsam has a South-east Asian source. Countless tonnes of natural flotsam would also have found its way to these lonely islands. Huge trees, ripped from tropical shores during wild storms, could have brought with them numerous seeds, creepers, flowering plants, insects, birds and reptiles as they floated across the open ocean like miniature islands of life. Wood-Jones (1910) reported the water-borne arrival of two crocodiles, several snakes and what was said to be a Maori war canoe. All had travelled on the dominant westward flowing current that draws in waters from the Indonesian archipelago, and northern and western Australia.

Mere arrival at an atoll, however, is no guarantee of successful colonisation. Even today the seeds of plants not normally seen on Cocos continue to be washed ashore. They are unable to take hold, however, as the conditions do not suit them. It has been suggested that the patch of mangroves on Horsburgh Island may have begun when early settlers tossed their seeds from the beach into the nearby swamp.

As well as wind-borne and water-borne plants and animals, the Cocos atolls also boast a large number of 'assisted passage immigrants' — species that have taken hold here as a direct consequence of the human settlement of the islands.

INTRODUCED SPECIES

It could be said that those species which humans have tried to establish on the Cocos (Keeling) Islands have not done as well as those they brought with them by accident.

The early settlers introduced sheep, goats, pigs, deer, rabbits, cats, dogs, a monkey, a lemur and several species of birds. Unfortunately, every ship that plied the waters of the Far East also carried a cargo of ants, cockroaches, beetles, scorpions, crickets, centipedes, mosquitoes, flies and rats. All found their way to Cocos.

The Cocos rats have the unique distinction of beating the first settlers to the islands. The shipwreck of the *Mauritius* in 1825 left its rodent survivors on an island the Cocos Malay people call *Pulu Tikus* ('rat island' — now Direction Island). In 1878 the wreck of the *Robert Portner* precipitated a second invasion by rats. The new arrivals spread to all the islands in the southern atoll and caused considerable damage in the coconut plantation. Sadly, these rats, together with copra beetles, centipedes and the tiny Fire Ants have proved to be some of the islands' most successful immigrant species.

The introduction of exotic plants such as the tomato, pea and numerous tropical fruits has been matched in almost every case by the consequent arrival of their specific parasites. These insect species might have happened upon the islands in the past, but died for want of their specific host. Moths and other plant-eating insects have been blown out to sea by storms, have become attracted to a passing ship's lights and have 'hitched a ride' to the vessel's destination.

Following his visit in 1830, four years after the settlement of the atoll, Commander A. A. Sandilands reported a wide variety of imported plants. These included the custard apple, tamarind, papaya, sugar cane, corn, numerous Asian vegetables, feed grasses for animals, oranges, figs, bananas and roses. The atoll's only reptiles, three species of gecko and a blind snake, may have been introduced at this time. Every imported species could quite possibly have been accompanied by its own brand of parasite or disease. Today a series of quarantine laws applies to all fruit, vegetable and animal matter entering and leaving the territory.

The combination of animal and plant species that is found on the atoll today is thus the product of a long history of chance arrival and a recent history of environmental modification.

Man's indelible influence on the Cocos-Keeling ecosystem is immediately obvious from the first glimpses of the islands out of the window of an approaching aircraft. The southern atoll has undergone a total transformation of vegetation in its short century and a half of settlement. Any remnants of earlier forests were dealt their final blows by the advent of the bulldozer. The last stands of Ironwood were felled and pushed out to sea in the 1960s. Only a few, massive, upturned stumps remain to give us some idea of their former stature. Nature had her revenge in 1968 when Cyclone Doreen ripped out the majority of the islands' planted palms. Subsequent replanting has now obliterated almost any hint of the islands' original condition.

Mangroves (*Rhizophora stylosa*) growing in the brackish lake on Horsburgh Island

Turbulent History

3

The drama of history loses nothing by reason of the smallness of its stage . . .

F. Wood-Jones describing Cocos in 1905.

DISCOVERY

Credit for the discovery of the Cocos (Keeling) Islands has long been attributed to Captain William Keeling of the East India Company in 1609. Historians have linked his homeward voyage from Bantam in the Dutch East Indies at that time and the subsequent charting of these islands. Strangely, it seems Keeling himself made no mention of the atoll in his own account of the journey.

The islands were certainly unrecorded prior to 1609. Ortelius' atlas, *Theatrum Orbis Terrarum*, published in Amsterdam in 1606, makes no mention of the atoll. A manuscript map drawn up in 1622 by Hessel Gerritsz shows a group he called 'Cocos Eylanden'. Robert Dudley's *Arcano del Mare* (1645–46) shows the islands and notes they were 'discovered by the English'. A large atlas published in Amsterdam in 1659 refers to the 'Cocos Islands', a name also adopted on French maps of the time.

William Dampier, on a voyage from the west coast of Australia in March 1688, intended to put in at the 'Cocos Islands' on his way to Sumatra but he was blown well off course. Instead, he recorded the first known landing on Christmas Island, 900 km to the north-east. Thornton, the English hydrographer, uses the name Kelling Island in his *Oriental Navigation* publication of 1703. Other British hydrographers of the time variously referred to the northern Cocos atoll as Keeling, Killing or North Keeling.

The first detailed description of the islands appeared in Dutch in 1753 in Van Keulen's *Zeefakkel*. They are described as low-lying, surrounded by reef and possessed of an inner lagoon and an abundance of coconuts. This

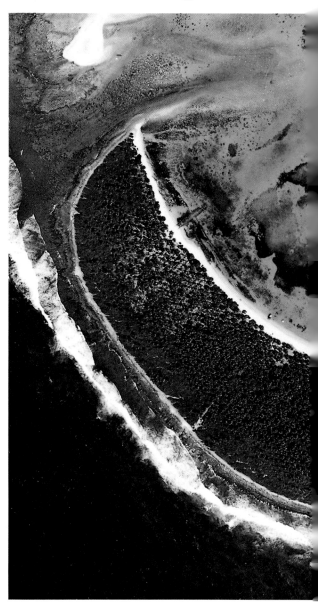

atlas also included a map of the southern atoll by Jan de Marre (1729-30). Merchantmen of the time referred to the group as the 'Triangular Islands'.

The title of 'Cocos-Keeling Islands' was bestowed by the British hydrographer, James Horsburgh, who compiled a detailed sailing directory of these waters in 1805. However, the early settlers called their atoll the 'Borneo

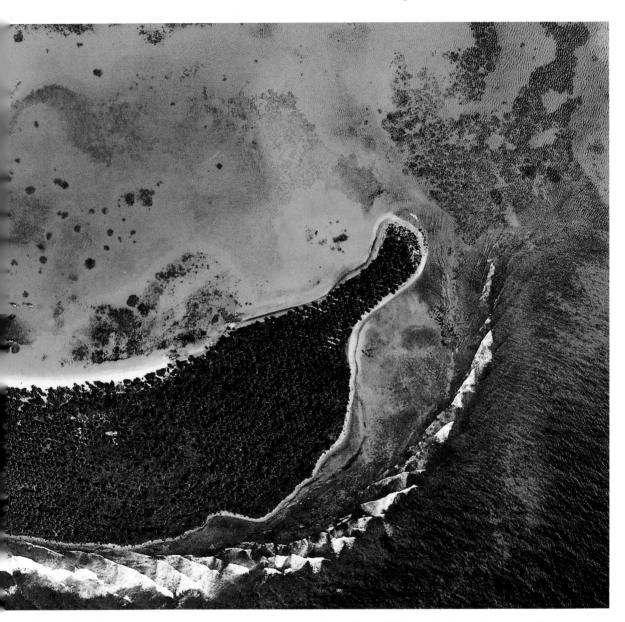

Coral Reefs' after their supply vessel, and later they used the name 'Keeling-Cocos Islands'. Colonial reports of the time accepted Horsburgh's title and the tiny outpost was subsequently called 'Cocos-Keeling' right up until 1955 when it acquired its current, bracketed, title.

Two hundred and seventeen years elapsed between Keeling's purported sighting of the atoll in 1609 and its ultimate settlement by Alexander Hare in 1826. A few passing navigators made reference to the islands but no accounts of landings were recorded until 1825 when a French brig, the *Mauritius*, met an untimely end on the reefs behind Direction Island. Captain Le Cour and his crew made it ashore and were rescued after a number of months.

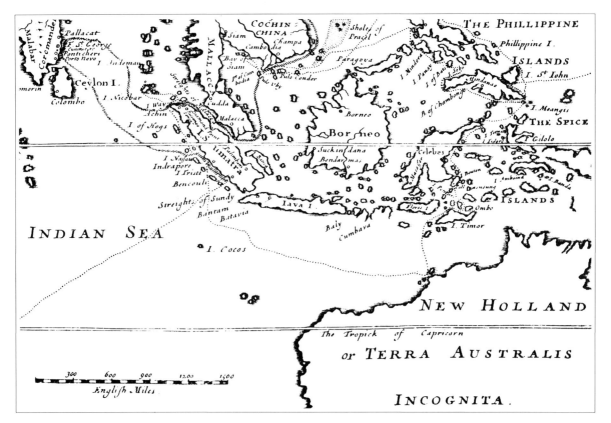

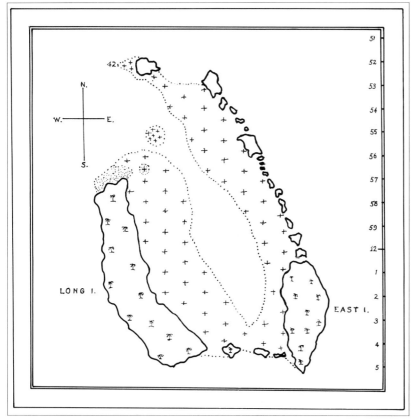

Above: English map of the East Indies showing part of William Dampier's route in 1688

Left: Early Dutch chart of Keeling Atoll (Van Keulen, 1753)

Captain Driscoll of the British brig, *Lonach*, called into the atoll on 24 November 1825 and reported the remains of a wreck. He and his crewmen spotted a large mast and bowsprit, a wooden barrel and a population of rats. Twelve days later Captain John Clunies Ross arrived in the islands and found the remains of the huts that the stranded sailors had built, several water pits and Arabic carvings on a number of trees.

The islands were quite a problem for seafarers in the early nineteenth century. On 15 December 1826 the English brig, *Sir Francis Nicholas Burton*, was wrecked on the southern shore of West Island and a number of lives were lost. In 1827 a Dutch corvette, the *Anna Paulowna*, was sent from Batavia to inspect the islands — but the commanding officer was unable to find them! The *Earl of Liverpool*, another British brig, was wrecked on the north-eastern shore of North Keeling in 1834. Her crew was saved, but most of her Singaporean cargo bound for London was lost.

BACKGROUND TO THE SETTLEMENT OF COCOS

To fully appreciate the circumstances of the settlement of Cocos it is necessary to examine the political climate in Europe and South-east Asia at the beginning of the nineteenth century. Europe at this time was being torn apart by the Napoleonic Wars. At the same time, Britain was assuming control over most of the Dutch overseas colonies in order to prevent them from falling into French hands.

In 1809 the Dutch abandoned Banjarmasin, their only settlement on the island of Borneo. The local Sultan was greatly alarmed by this development, as Dutch sponsorship had elevated his political and economic status well above that of the other sultans in southern Borneo. By a stroke of good fortune an astute British merchant from Malacca visited the Sultan during this difficult time. He was Alexander Hare, a man with self-seeking but romantic ambitions.

A few months later Hare introduced the Sultan's representatives to a friend of his, none other than Stamford Raffles, Agent to the Governor-General of the Malay States. At this time Raffles was planning a British occupation of the Netherlands East Indies. He had read widely about Borneo and was well aware of the fact that the Dutch had clearly abandoned Banjarmasin. This meant that any colonies the British might establish in Borneo should outlive any subsequent peace treaty with the Dutch.

Raffles became the British Lieutenant-Governor of Java in 1811 and he appointed Alexander Hare as British Resident of Banjarmasin in 1812. Hare was to work closely with the Sultan in reducing piracy and regulating local trade. He managed to negotiate a treaty between the British East India Company and the Sultan that was hailed in Java as a great diplomatic triumph. Raffles chose to overlook the fact that, at the same time, Alexander Hare had also made a private treaty with the Sultan. This gave Hare the sovereign rights over an area some 1400 square miles in extent. He was thus British Resident on behalf of the East India Company and a sovereign prince. In 1815 he was promoted further by Raffles to the position of Political Commissioner-General of Borneo. He had his own flag, struck his own coinage and was the first Englishman to become known as a 'White Rajah'.

The new colony began with great enthusiasm. Hare was determined to make the venture profitable for all concerned — the Sultan, the Company and himself. At the same time he was revelling in the pleasures of being an eastern potentate.

He was given a number of staff to work with. His immediate assistant was a Dutchman named Van der Wahl, who later proved to be totally unreliable. In addition to him were a detachment of Malay Police, two doctors, some clerks and an assortment of craftsmen and coolies. He was also joined in Banjarmasin by a number of adventurous and ambitious Europeans, one of whom was a seafarer named John Clunies Ross. This young Scotsman was subsequently given the position of Banjarmasin Harbour-master.

By 1813 Raffles had succeeded in making treaties with a number of other sultans in

Pulu Maria from
West Island

coastal areas of Borneo. He foresaw that Java might well be returned to the Dutch in time, but believed that his arrangements in Borneo would survive. These would provide Britain

man, Lord Moira, was alarmed by Raffles' ideas. He believed that with the ultimate return of the Dutch there would be a degree of hostility towards any new British settlements in the region. It would be too costly for the British to defend them, for they were already fully committed to the Indian subcontinent and had no desire to extend their responsibilities any further east. Besides, the British were keen to remain on friendly terms with the Dutch.

In August 1814, the long-expected treaty between Britain and the Netherlands was signed and the Dutch were given back the colonies they had held in 1803. Java passed back into their control, and ultimately Borneo followed suit in 1817.

Hare was bitterly disappointed with the British authorities. To add insult to injury, his Banjarmasin enterprise had not proven very successful. He had found a great deal of trouble in recruiting the kind of labour he required to work in his sugar, pepper and coffee plantations and had arranged with Raffles for some 3000 Javanese convicts to be sent across to him. The Sultan was unhappy with the effect that these undesirables were having on his subjects. It seems that Hare had put too much energy into building himself a palace and filling it with luxury items and servants. He was too fond of holidays on his other estates in Java and had often left his struggling settlement in the hands of his brother, John, the untrustworthy Van der Wahl and the young Clunies Ross.

In 1818 the Sultan of Banjarmasin declared that he had lost his copy of the treaty with Hare and went ahead with a new one with the Dutch. He then refused to keep any of Hare's labourers on his lands. In the absence of any records as to whether Hare's workers were free men or convicts, all had to be shipped back to Java. Here they created immense legal and administrative problems for the incoming Dutch government.

Hare had been abandoned by the British East India Company and the Sultan. He now began to petition the new Dutch authorities

with the beginnings of a commercial empire in the East Indies. Unfortunately, the appointment of a new Governor-General of the Malay States in 1813 upset Raffles' plans. The new

to compensate him with an estate in Java. All his pleadings were in vain.

John Hare and John Clunies Ross left Banjarmasin in the *Borneo*, a 428-ton ship that the latter had built for the trading 'House of Hare'. They joined Alexander briefly in Java, but the authorities there were growing weary of his continual complaints and finally expelled him from the country in 1820. With the brothers Hare and a large number of Alexander's retainers on board, the *Borneo* sailed for the Cape of Good Hope. There Alexander hoped to recover from a serious illness and renegotiate his status with the Dutch authorities. He had with him 42 men, 43 women and 27 children and he moved onto a large farm near Capetown. Clunies Ross sailed home to England where he continued to work for the House of Hare.

On a subsequent trading mission out of London in the *Borneo*, Clunies Ross again met Alexander Hare in Capetown harbour in 1825. Hare was aboard the *Hippomenes* with John's brother, Robert Clunies Ross, in command. He had been unable to settle his Banjarmasin grievances with the Dutch authorities and was determined to get away from them and settle on an island in the Indian Ocean.

John Clunies Ross left Capetown and proceeded on his trading assignment to the East Indies. On his homeward journey he had orders to investigate Christmas Island on Alexander Hare's behalf as a possible site for a settlement. Bad weather forced him to abandon these plans. He was still able to survey the Cocos-Keeling Islands, however, and there he took soundings, charted the entrance to the lagoon, roughly mapped the circle of islands and planted a few fruit trees on Horsburgh and Direction Islands.

On his return to the Cape he learned that Alexander Hare had finally left the port after months of waiting in the harbour. Robert Clunies Ross had apparently delivered him and approximately one hundred other people to the Cocos-Keeling Islands in May 1826. There he had had established a settlement on Home Island and set up subsidiary camps on most of the other major islands.

Hare did not initially plan to stay very long on the atoll. It was to be a temporary measure while he waited to negotiate his return to his estates in Java. As the prospects of his return diminished, however, a longer term view for the new settlement developed. At first the major aim was to cultivate sufficient food to feed his residents. He later turned to the extraction of coconut oil for export.

Back in London, the House of Hare was suffering badly from a number of Alexander's outstanding accounts with the East India Company. John Clunies Ross offered to take charge of Hare's people on Cocos, to allow him time to settle his affairs. He was given the power of attorney by Hare's brothers and left England in 1826 with his family. He intended to set up a ship refitting service on the islands and to convince Alexander Hare to return to England.

When John Clunies Ross arrived at Cocos, Hare was furious that his passengers were not the overseers he had asked his brothers to send him. Instead they were settlers brought by Clunies Ross himself to work on an entirely different project. The machinery Hare had ordered had also failed to materialise. As to the suggestion that he should return home, Hare was adamant that he was going to remain on the islands. He made what he could of the environment and in 1829 the *Borneo* took several tons of coconut oil to England.

Clunies Ross had originally set up a camp on *Pulu Gangsa* (Goose Island), the island immediately to the north of Hare's settlement, but as the tension between them began to mount he moved his party down to South Island. Here he called his tiny settlement New Selma, after the legendary ancient capital of the kingdom of Scotland.

Hare had already set up garden-settlements on West, Horsburgh and Direction Islands and enjoyed a windy retreat on Prison Island. The initial composition of his group is not known, but a report by Van der Jagt, who visited the islands in November 1829, noted 36 men, 25 women and 37 children — a total of 98 persons.

This group represented all that was left of Hare's entourage that had begun in Banjarmasin. It was predominantly Malay with a number of people of Chinese, Papuan and Indian descent. It is believed that the party also contained a few African and Papuan individuals. The people came from such places as Bali, Bima, Celebes, Madura, Sumbawa, Timor, Sumatra, Pasir-Kutai, Malacca, Penang, Batavia, Cerebon, Banjarmasin, Pontianak, Tasikmalaya and Kota Waringan. They were described by subsequent visitors to the islands as being nominally Moslem and speaking Malay — the trading *lingua franca* of the East Indies.

The wreck of the brig *Sir Francis Nicholas Burton*, in December 1826, was the first event to disturb Hare's privacy on Cocos. Hare supported the surviving crew until the subsequent arrival of Clunies Ross. One sailor, Charles

High school students learn about their islands' history beside the grave of Suma, a settler who arrived in 1826

43

Downie, elected to remain with Hare and another sailor, Henry Keld, joined the Clunies Ross party.

Hare and Clunies Ross, his former employee, found themselves in a situation that neither of them could tolerate. They began to taunt each other. In an assessment of possible coconut yields from the atoll in 1828 Hare purposely included the island on which Clunies Ross had settled. In return, Clunies Ross proposed a sharing out of the available land which gave him a larger proportion than Hare was willing to concede. Both knew that Clunies Ross had the backing of the Hare brothers in London, but Alexander was not going to leave the islands as there was no one he felt he could trust to look after his interests.

Towards the end of 1828 the *Hippomenes* passed through Cocos again. From those aboard Hare was able to secure the services of Arthur Keating and Norman Ogilvie. Keating left a year later with Charles Downie, but Ogilvie seemed to like the place and became Hare's overseer on Direction Island. The commercial extraction of coconut oil for export began under his direction.

Hare's people were still slaves to all intents and purposes, despite their Dutch certificates of emancipation. All had signed themselves and their children over to Hare as 'property' and depended on him absolutely. They were allocated work on the various fruit and vegetable patches that were established on West, Horsburgh and Direction Islands. Their living conditions were spartan and their food rations meagre. Hare kept any children in his own household, along with a number of personal attendants. Adult workers received one coconut-shell's amount of rice per person per day. Their annual clothing allocation was a pair of trousers and a shirt for the men and one sarong and a kabaya for the women. Children were not clothed until they were old enough to work.

It is not certain when Hare moved his own camp from Home Island to Prison Island, but it appears to have been in response to harassment of his female companions by members of the Clunies Ross party. By 1830 it seems that Hare was growing increasingly despondent and decidedly eccentric.

Clunies Ross' move to South Island in 1827 had provided him with a measure of distance from his rival, but his settlement suffered badly from a shortage of labour and too great a distance from the deep anchorage he called Port Albion. Between 1828 and 1830 a number of his workers decided to leave and his plans for a trading depot looked destined to fail. He desperately needed Hare's labour force to work for him. The only way to oust their 'master' was to discredit him with his brothers and with those to whom he was appealing for assistance.

At one stage Hare petitioned the British Prime Minister, Lord Canning, regarding his desire to return to his Java estates. Clunies Ross was well aware of Lord Canning's strong anti-slavery feelings and presented a dark picture of Alexander's settlement to the House of Hare in London.

Sun-dried copra, mainstay of the Cocos economy for most of the islands' history

Great lengths were taken to portray the man who was once his employer as a cruel, demented rogue in the eyes of the outside world. In 1828 a document of Hare's, destined for his brothers in London, was extensively tampered with to create the impression that its author was unbalanced and suffering from delusions of grandeur.

In 1831 the House of Hare was in deep financial trouble, so Alexander went to Batavia and left the islands in the hands of Ogilvie. He never returned. In 1834 word reached the atoll that he had died in Java. Coincidentally, Ogilvie was drowned in a mishap off North Keeling a little later in that same year.

The Clunies Ross settlement on South Island originally comprised 21 people, only one of whom was Javanese. There were ten English tradesmen in the party (five apprentices, two carpenters, two boatmen and a blacksmith), a cook, a houseboy, a maidservant and eight members of the Clunies Ross family. In 1829 the total population of the atoll was 175, with 20 Europeans and 155 people from the Indies, New Guinea and the Cape. By 1830 Clunies Ross' mother-in-law had died and ten of his workers had left on passing ships. Only one of the tradesmen, an apprentice named William Leisk, remained on South Island.

In 1834 John Clunies Ross moved his small group to Home Island, assumed control over Hare's people and turned his attention towards the islands' coconut palms. He substituted a number of Javanese seamen for his departed Scots and these, together with William Leisk, taught the islanders to build sailing ships. Their first project, a schooner called the *Harriet*, was built on South Island and launched in 1835.

At first, whole coconuts were exported to Mauritius and Singapore and coconut oil to Java. Later trade focused on copra and oil, with Java as the most important market. By 1837 Clunies Ross had succeeded in recovering his original investment. His increasing prosperity was boosted by the visits of numerous whaling vessels on their return from trips to the Southern Ocean.

Unfortunately, the crews of these vessels played havoc in the Cocos community.

One crewman deserted from the *Trusty* in January 1836. His name was Joseph Raymond, and he was an American, whom Clunies Ross later accused of having a criminal past. It would seem his major 'crime' was to question the circumstances of Norman Ogilvie's death, an event still fresh in the minds of the Malay workforce. Raymond was soon befriended by a disillusioned William Leisk and together they set about opposing Clunies Ross' authority.

They overcharged a Dutch ship and allowed whaling crews their way with the island women. Raymond instigated a strike for higher pay and a reduction in working hours. There was a spate of arson and talk of the possible seizure of the *Harriet*. No wonder a visiting Charles Darwin in April 1836 wrote of the workers' 'discontented state'. Clunies Ross was away at the time of this historic visit by the *Beagle*, unaware of the plotting going on in his absence. Immediately upon his return he wrote a lengthy document justifying his management of the settlement, vehemently refuting the visitors' veiled suggestions of slave-keeping.

John Clunies Ross became so concerned about the unsettling developments that he went to Trincomalee in Ceylon, for help. He arrived there in June 1837 and discussed the situation with Admiral Sir T. Bladen Capel. The admiral responded by sending Commander Harding of H.M. sloop, *Pelorus*, to visit the atoll in December of that year. This visit was significant in many ways. It not only managed to solve the problems presented by Leisk and Raymond, but it also contributed to a better deal for the Cocos workers and produced the first census of the islands' population (see Appendix). In addition, it shed some light on the difficulties that John Clunies Ross was having in getting his claims for British sovereignty recognised.

Commander Harding was able to secure a full and detailed apology from Raymond and

Leisk and negotiated a pardon for them so long as they left the islands. He also arranged return passages for any Cocos families who wished to be repatriated, and persuaded Clunies Ross to help them financially. Harding helped to draw up a formal code of law and order for the settlement and guaranteed an increase in the workers' daily wage. His report spoke most respectfully of John Clunies Ross, in terms befitting the full attention of the colonial authorities to his claims for British sovereignty. This last was the only point on which Harding failed. The Colonial Office was not interested in extending their responsibilities to this tiny outpost in the Indian Ocean.

The inner shells are split and the fleshy copra is extracted

CONSOLIDATION

In 1842 Captain Clunies Ross' brother, James, came to settle on Cocos. It seems that the last years of John's life were mainly spent writing lengthy justifications of his settlement and in refuting comments made by a number of influential visitors to the islands. He petitioned both the Dutch and British authorities relentlessly in his drive to gain official recognition for his settlement. The community grew steadily in number and references began to be made to the 'Cocos Malay' people. Apart from members of his own family and a few Javanese seamen and their wives, there was no importation of outside labour during his time.

Captain Clunies Ross' eldest son, John George, had come to the islands at the age of four and had gone to sea at an early age. He only travelled to England once in his life, preferring instead to travel through the East Indies. He lived in Java from 1838 to 1844 and this entitled him to Dutch citizenship and the right to fly a Dutch flag on his ship. In 1841 he met and married a Javanese girl named Supia Dupong and returned to Cocos.

In the light of his own background in the Netherlands East Indies and his son's naturalisation, John Clunies Ross decided to fly a Dutch flag on Cocos in 1841, but when news of this reached the Netherlands he was asked to take it down. It seemed that no one was interested in the islands.

Captain John Clunies Ross died in 1854 and John George, then 31, assumed control of the problematic settlement and his father's debts.

Very few official visitors came to the islands after Harding's memorable stay in 1837. When the British man-o'-war, the *H.M. Juno*, arrived in the lagoon on 31 March 1857, John George Clunies Ross was away in Java. His uncle James could hardly believe what followed — the islands were finally going to be annexed to Britain after 31 years of petitioning. Captain Fremantle presented the official papers to James Clunies Ross, who duly signed them on his nephew's behalf. The *Juno* remained on Cocos for three months until Fremantle eventually met the man he had designated as 'Governor'. Great celebrations followed. All on Cocos were oblivious to the fact that the annexation itself was actually an enormous bureaucratic blunder.

Thirty years later the Colonial Office admitted that they had made a very serious mistake in annexing the Cocos-Keeling Islands. Fremantle's entire mission was a series of errors. He was sent to claim the Cocos Islands in the Andaman group to the north, when in actual fact they had already been annexed to Britain. His instructions were sufficiently vague that he went instead to the Cocos-Keeling Islands and made John George Clunies Ross a very happy man.

The annexation gave the Cocos settlers the necessary impetus to begin in earnest to develop the islands as a coconut plantation. Its owner, as a governor under the crown, was to be held responsible for the conduct of the colony. J. G. Clunies Ross spent a great deal of time thereafter recording and codifying the local laws that had been drawn up by Commander Harding in 1837. He also began the practice of importing workers from Bantam in Java.

The only men who could be engaged for long-term service outside Java were chain-gang criminals. John George Clunies Ross made arrangements with the Batavian authorities to provide work for convicts who were serving the last year of their sentences. After one year on Cocos they were to be given the option of returning to Java or of staying on Cocos and calling for a suitable marriage partner. These convict labourers were later described by John George's son as "capable of any atrocity" and as a "turbulent set of men".

Coconut husking is a back-breaking task

They were housed in a separate *kampong* (village) from the Cocos Malay people and this system of recruitment continued for 20 years. The convicts outnumbered the permanent residents and many did not take kindly to exile on the lonely islands on which they found themselves.

Every night the Cocos Malay residents maintained an armed guard and signalled changes in the watch by ringing a bell. The crime most feared was arson. At a fixed hour each evening, every Cocos resident had to report to the guardhouse. No fires were to be lit after sunset and no one was permitted to stay overnight on other islands. All boats were numbered and had to be in their correct places by sunset. Any disappearances of boats or people prompted an immediate search.

Many of the convicts took to their heels and went missing for weeks at a time. There were plenty of dramas when certain characters were 'at large' and likely to raid people's homes for food. No coined money was allowed and the local currency consisted of tiny sheepskin promissory notes signed by Clunies Ross.

Token currency used on the islands:
Top left: ¼ Rupee sheepskin note, 1879
Top right: 1 Rupee paper note, 1902
Centre left: 5 Rupee ivory token, 1910
Centre right: 1 Rupee ivory token, 1913
Bottom left: 25 cents ivory token, 1910
Bottom right: 2 Rupee ivory token, 1913
(*Courtesy: Cocos Museum*)

During the 1860s there was a disagreement that led to a riot and the destruction of J. G. Clunies Ross' house. In 1870 an uprising followed a murder and the ringleader was locked up and later deported. In 1874 a group of convicts stole one of the Clunies Ross' boats, but they were pursued and recaptured.

A disastrous cyclone struck the islands in 1862 and Clunies Ross' eldest son, George, was recalled from studies in England to assist in the rebuilding of the community and the islands' economy. John George Clunies Ross died in 1871 and his son, George, assumed control at the age of 29.

One of George's first actions after the passing of his father was to terminate the convict labour scheme. In this he was assisted by a change of law in Batavia that allowed him to import Bantamese 'coolies' (see Appendix). The curfew-system and the placement of all-night guards still continued, however.

In 1876 the islands were struck by a second, more severe, cyclone. Visitors to the islands reported that reconstruction and replanting work proceeded at a strapping pace under the energetic leadership of George Clunies Ross.

Bantamese labourers were still being recruited for terms of three to ten years and they were given a small plot of land in their own *kampong* on which they could construct a house. Rudimentary building materials were supplied and weekly food and firewood rations were allocated. They had to work ten hours per day for six days each week. For the daily collection of 400 coconuts the contractors were paid one Cocos rupee. On top of this they earned an extra eight rupees per month as wages. Those contracted labourers who had been on the islands for more than a year were offered incentives for the collection of extra nuts. Those who were fortunate to be 'Cocos-born' were paid roughly twice these amounts. Very little of this was cash-in-hand. An account was kept for each worker at the store which recorded all credits and debits. Whenever contracted labourers decided to return to Java they were presented with their balance. This was often in the form of a promissory note to the relevant authorities.

George Clunies Ross commenced an enormous coconut planting programme. He established a blacksmithing workshop and imported the latest in copra processing machinery. Brick storehouses were built and large kilns were set up to produce lime from coral rubble. Trolley-lines criss-crossed Home Island for ease of transport, a series of breakwaters were constructed, boating channels dredged and the family home was rebuilt in grand style with tiles and bricks from Scotland. In 1885 George sailed his own schooner to England and back. Three years later he and his brother, Andrew, established the first settlement on Christmas Island. George Clunies Ross' boat-building skills were put to good use as the islanders were taught to make large trading boats and smaller sailing craft. The trading boats brought back rice, spices, cloth, turtles and brides from Java. Economically, the estate began to prosper.

The islanders themselves did not share greatly in the prosperity, however, as malnutrition and dysentery took their toll on Cocos Malay families. Between 1880 and 1885, 35 out of the 57 recorded deaths were due to beriberi. This vitamin deficiency was regarded at the time as a contagious disease and groups of sufferers were placed on South Island and North Keeling as though they were lepers. Frequent outbreaks of dysentery were either attributed to the vagaries of the wind or to the vegetation-clearing programme. Infant mortality was high and child mortality was increasing. The islanders' diet was clearly deficient, sanitation was inadequate and working conditions were such that mothers spent insufficient time with their youngsters. In 1901 no less than 33 out of the 40 recorded deaths in the estate were those of infants (see Appendix).

In 1906 twelve discontented Bantamese labourers achieved the seemingly impossible feat of escaping from Cocos and reaching Ceringin, Java, after 45 days at sea. Led by N'tong, a skilled celestial navigator, and his friend Umal Songgeng, the group reached their destination in the *Palace*, a yacht they stole from the estate. After this embarrassing event, George Clunies Ross decreed that all rudders belonging to every sailing vessel had to be locked up each night and collected again the following morning.

Despite the dire circumstances of its inhabitants, the estate continued to ride on a wave of prosperity. It had no difficulty in selling its copra, whole coconuts, coconut oil and Mengkudu wood (*Morinda citrifolia*) to Batavia right up until the disastrous cyclone of 1909. An economic recession that has implications even today then descended over the islands. The cyclone broke George Clunies Ross' spirit and he died in England a year later. The vicious storm is said to have blown down or decapitated 90 per cent of the atoll's coconut palms. It left only five of the 110 houses in the two villages standing and severely damaged *Oceania House*, the Clunies Ross family mansion.

Oceania House, residence of the Clunies-Ross family, built in 1893

A VITAL LINK TO THE WORLD

Up until the turn of the century the inhabitants of Cocos rarely saw individuals from the outside world. Their contacts were restricted to government officials, lone adventurers or the crews of passing ships. In 1901 the Eastern Extension Telegraph Company established a relay station on Direction Island for their underwater cable network. In 1910 this was supplemented by a wireless unit to keep the cable station in regular contact with passing ships.

This once obscure atoll was destined to become a vital link in world communications of the early twentieth century. One submarine cable was laid to the south-west to South Africa, another north to Singapore and a third to Perth in Western Australia. The company leased approximately half of Direction Island and built a number of bungalows and offices. Staff in the early days of operation numbered up to 40, about half of whom were Chinese domestics from Singapore. A doctor was included among the residents and he acted as a consultant to the Clunies Ross Estate.

George Clunies Ross was wary of the effect the new settlement might have on his workforce, so he restricted their opportunities for contact with it. Europeans at the Cable Station were not allowed access to the two villages but were regularly invited to Oceania House. Any Cocos Malay workers who went to Direction Island were closely supervised.

A murder at the Cable Station in 1902 revealed a glaring anomaly in the law and order situation on Cocos. A Chinese employee of the station was sent to Singapore to stand trial for the murder of another Chinese worker. The Attorney-General of the Straits Settlements found that he had no jurisdiction over the islands in this matter and the accused was set free.

George Clunies Ross set up his own 'court' on Home Island, comprising four headmen, four elders and himself. Subsequent sentences passed by this body ranged from fines and floggings to hard labour.

The cable station on Direction Island, 1960 (*Courtesy J. Hand*)

The *J. G. Clunies Ross*, a much-valued Cocos-built schooner, was reported missing in 1892 after it had been lent to the rather unsavoury crew of an Italian ship. Their vessel, the *Luigi Raffo*, was wrecked on the reef and the stranded crewmen were proving quite a problem in the settlement. Then the *Broughton*, a partly-insured barque belonging to the estate, was severely damaged in 1902 and became a total loss. The burden of the cyclone in 1909 was almost more than the settlement could bear, as it came hard on the heels of financial set-backs in Batavia.

George Clunies Ross died on the Isle of Wight in England in 1910. A year later, eight Cocos Malay seamen travelled to England to collect a new schooner, the *Rainbow*, and sail her home with the exhumed body of George Clunies Ross aboard. The Malay crew were not told the nature of their cargo until their eventual return to the islands. The trip home was plagued by storm after storm, two changes of captain and it took far longer than anticipated. All the way back the Cocos Malay sailors were under the impression that their precious cargo was a grand piano!

In 1912 George's son, John Sydney, assumed control of the settlement and added a hyphen to his surname. He headed a murder trial on Home Island that resulted in the imposition of the death sentence. The two accused, Aspin and Sah'it, were found guilty of the murder of Ra'isan and were subsequently dispatched into the ocean behind Horsburgh Island with heavy weights around their ankles.

Not long afterwards, Natan bin Dahem became inconsolable after the cruel whipping of his son, Kembrin, by Edmund Clunies Ross. He left the estate with his family and some friends in 1913 and resettled in Singapore. This group included Beppo bin Wahit and Agnan bin Reji'i who went on to England, signed up with the British Army and Navy respectively and fought in World War One.

The war with Germany put the Cocos Islands on the world map in 1914 with the sinking of the German cruiser, *S.M.S. Emden*, and the theft of the estate's three-masted schooner, the *Ayesha*, by a German raiding party. The war compensation received for this loss was insufficient to replace her and John Sydney Clunies-Ross was forced to sell off another of his vessels at the time because of her German origins.

There was insufficient manpower to completely clear the 1909 cyclone debris or to replant the plantation in a coordinated fashion. All able-bodied men were fully occupied in rebuilding the *kampong*. Consequently many new palms had an opportunity to sprout among the storm debris. These grew too closely to one another and became poor producers of nuts. Copra prices plummeted after the war and Sydney Clunies-Ross was forced to rely heavily on his dividends from phosphate mining on Christmas Island to offset his losses on Cocos. In the space of just 20 years Sydney Clunies-Ross had accrued huge unpaid tax arrears and the estate was losing money heavily, leading to an enormous overdraft with the estate's Singapore agents.

Between the wars, the Malay community progressively rebuilt their village under Sydney's direction. The two *kampongs* were finally combined into one by the 1920s in a mammoth project which, unfortunately, also consumed a large proportion of the southern atoll's reserves of good wood. By 1941 the islands' population had risen to 1450 and food supply was becoming a pressing problem. The outbreak of World War II meant that supply ships were infrequent and unreliable, so severe rationing had to be imposed on the community. On several occasions the settlement ran completely out of rice and the islanders were forced to subsist on coconuts and fish.

Sydney Clunies-Ross lacked his father's drive and interest in the estate. He spent one out of every three years in England, lost the support of most members of his own family and continually left the estate in the hands of a succession of managers. An unguarded remark of his to the Press in London in 1936 drew the attention of the British Anti-Slavery League to conditions on Cocos. Fortunately for him, the advent of war and his own death a little later cut short the possibility of a detailed investigation. He did not marry until the age of 56 and it was only nine years before his young wife left him on Cocos and returned to England with the four children. She did not return to the islands until two years after Sydney's death and was not included in his original will. A series of swift legal moves was necessary for her to be included as one of his trustees.

The doctor from the Cable and Wireless Station described the Cocos Malay population as 'colourless and listless' in 1941. Nutrition was poor, there were few sources of stimulation and there seemed to be an aura of decay about the place. Dysentery and round worms were endemic and the workers knew nothing of the outside world. Even the very time of day was different from that in the neighbouring Direction Island. Sydney Clunies-Ross would set the Cocos clocks every day according to his own sextant readings! When World War II began, the Home Island *kampong* had 243 houses and there was a small settlement on Horsburgh Island.

The islanders were intrigued by the arrival of a detachment from the Ceylon Garrison Artillery later in that year. They had been sent to Cocos to set up and man two six-inch guns on Horsburgh Island in order to protect the cable station from a possible attack by the Japanese. A company of Ceylon Light Infantry was stationed on Direction Island for the same purpose. News from the Cable Station that Singapore had fallen to the Japanese in February 1942 and that a number of ex-Cocos Islanders had been killed further disturbed the Home Island population.

On 9 November 1960, 46 years after the sinking of the *SMS Emden*, Sir Charles Gairdner unveiled a plaque on Direction Island to commemorate the battle. Here he inspects a guard-of-honour from *HMAS Diamantina* (*Courtesy J. Hand*)

ISLAND PEACE SHATTERED

The Cocos Malay people's isolation from the events of the wider world was shattered on 3 March 1942, when Direction Island was shelled by a Japanese warship. Fortunately, the huge decoy fires that raged afterwards led the invaders into believing that they had succeeded in knocking out the relay station completely. The British authorities played along with this misinterpretation and the islands were never officially mentioned by name again for the rest of the war.

For the next three years, regular Japanese air-raid runs from occupied Java kept the Home Island community under pressure. A major bombing assault in August 1944 destroyed 27 houses and claimed the lives of two residents. Little regular copra work was achieved during these years as people were continually fleeing to other islands for their safety. Sydney Clunies-Ross became quite despondent about the situation and died of distress in 1944, shortly after the major bombing raid. The islands were soon placed under the control of a series of military administrators. The first, in August 1944, was Lieutenant-Colonel J. E. B. Jessamine.

Detachments from the British Army, Royal Navy and Royal Marines had already arrived and set up camp on Home Island. As the war situation developed several islanders were offered employment by the military and a small, but lucrative, bartering economy began. This grew into quite large proportions as time went on and sections of Oceania House were later transformed into a 'clearing house' for all manner of trade. Needless to say, the plantation declined further and the local economy became grossly unbalanced.

The conflict in the Asia-Pacific region was building to the point where the Allies felt that they needed an Indian Ocean air base. In March 1945 'Operation Cockroach' began and units from the Royal Air Force, Royal Indian Air Force and Fleet Air Arm began to arrive on Cocos by ship and commence the construction of a 2000 yard metallic airstrip on West Island.

Thousands of coconut palms were felled and bulldozed into the sea — to the utter amazement of the Cocos Malay people who were witnessing modern technology for the first time. The strip was operational in just two months and the first aircraft landed and refuelled in May 1945. The Cocos base was initially used for reconnaissance flights and the dropping of intelligence personnel into the Japanese-controlled East Indies. At the peak of operations there were 8300 military personnel on the atoll. Cocos was to have played an important role in a major assault on the enemy; however, a rapid turn-around in events saw the Japanese surrender in September 1945, and the Cocos airstrip was closed down in February of the following year — just twelve months after it had begun.

What an extraordinary year this had been for the isolated inhabitants of Home Island. Even at the close of operations, West Island still boasted over 3000 military. It took fourteen ships and six weeks to finally evacuate the 245 British Army, 256 Royal Indian Air Force, 445 Royal Air Force and 2215 Indian Army members who were the last to leave the islands. Much of their equipment was abandoned to the elements and it was during this time that the caretaker administration of Cocos passed from military into civilian hands.

The end of the war left Home Island reeling. The estate had lost its leadership and was in debt to the Singapore Government, the plantation had been neglected and the seemingly endless military rations were now starting to dwindle. On the other hand, people had gained new confidence and new knowledge about the wider world, and had new expectations. Improved health conditions had precipitated a marked decline in the death rate and the population had increased to 1814 by 1947. There was much confusion and debate about the future of the estate and its inhabitants. The military and civil administrators had tried to reorganise the plantation, but supplies were hard to obtain from war-torn Singapore and food had to be severely rationed.

The islanders hoped for some respite from the confusion with the return of Mrs Clunies-Ross and her son, John Cecil, in 1946. However their hopes were dashed by her fierce determination to make the islands pay. This led to her decision to drastically reduce the Malay population by promoting emigration. The Colonial Office in London could see the economic problem, but were more concerned about the islanders' ability to cope with transplantation into a different environment, far away from everything that was familiar to them. The islanders themselves plunged into deep despair when the reality of the situation dawned on them. For the next three years an official debate raged about possible locations and resettlement expenses.

At home in the Cocos *kampong*, relatives conducted their own emotional debates. Families were disintegrating and there were seven divorces in the 1949–1951 period. There had only been seven divorces recorded during the previous fifty years.

Home Islanders meet and trade with military personnel at Rumah Baru, West Island, 1945. (*Courtesy Imperial War Museum, London*)

In July 1947 a survey party of four, led by Hosman bin Awang, inspected Christmas Island, Singapore and several sites in peninsular Malaya. The group displayed some interest in the first two, but the jungles of Malaya did not appeal to them at all. Mrs Clunies-Ross' appointment of a most unpopular estate manager in 1947 hastened the emigration debate. In July 1948 there was a one-day strike. People went fishing and gathering coconuts for their own use. Bands of young men chopped down dozens of young palms to get at their nourishing centre-shoots. Emergency supplies were requested, but these took a further two months to arrive. The islands' population was increasing rapidly and Mrs Clunies-Ross announced that anyone who wanted to leave the islands and resettle on Christmas Island or Singapore would be helped to do so. A few families had already left for Singapore before the war and the idea was gaining in popularity.

News later came from the Singapore authorities that the Colonial Development Corporation of North Borneo needed labour to restore an abandoned Japanese estate near Tawau. Names of Cocos Malay people interested in any overseas destinations were submitted to the civil administrator. A small group, led by Hosman bin Awang, left for Christmas Island in 1948. The first group of 180 emigrants destined for Borneo left Cocos in late 1949. Four or five more batches of similar size left on the supply ship, the *T.S.S. Islander*, every six months during the next three years. Some opted to go to Christmas Island and Singapore, but the majority headed for North Borneo (now the Malaysian state of Sabah).

The emigrants and their families dreaded the arrival of the ship. Those who left were transported as deck passengers and many became seriously ill. Adelin binte Kalwie, the daughter of a former headman, contracted pneumonia during the November 1949 passage and died. A number of others died during their two-week transit stop in Singapore. Departures from Cocos were so emotional that the ship's captain later opted to leave at night to spare his passengers the agony of seeing their homeland disappear over the horizon.

The new settlers were greatly disappointed by North Borneo. The climate was different. They were a long way from the sea. The work was hard and many died from malaria and other new diseases. Several went mad in their strange new environment and Rojeman binte Remi'in hanged herself in a fit of depression. Small groups continued to transfer from one overseas settlement to another. The emotional upheavals of these transfers still have their repercussions today, as reunions are made with 'long lost' friends and relations.

Top left:
Residents of Home Island marvel at modern technology — a Spitfire aircraft assembled on Cocos from boxed components, 1945.
(*Courtesy Imperial War Museum, London*)

Bottom left:
Spitfires lined up on the West Island runway, 1945
(*Courtesy Imperial War Museum, London*)

ENTER AUSTRALIA

In 1951 an agreement was made in principle for the transfer of the islands from Britain to Australia and a full reconstruction of the wartime airstrip was begun. By mid-1952 the territory was back on the world map as QANTAS, and later South African Airways, used the islands for a transit-stop on the long haul between Perth, Western Australia, and Johannesburg in South Africa.

Most outside interest in the islands centred on the airstrip and there was little close scrutiny of events and conditions on Home Island. By the end of 1951 only 350 Cocos Malay people were left. This group included only 70 able-bodied men and it took quite a deal of persuasion to stop them from leaving as well. John Cecil Clunies-Ross had to offer them new housing, electric lights and increased pay to convince them to stay.

The islands were formally detached from the British Colony of Singapore and accepted by Australia as a territory on 23 November, 1955.

Repairs to a QANTAS passenger aircraft, 1960 (*Courtesy J. Hand*)

It appeared as though things had settled down. The Malay population grew steadily and had climbed to 460 by June 1957. Suddenly trouble brewed again. The outward cause was a food shortage, but behind this was the unwelcome return of the same despised manager whose actions had helped to divide the community in 1948. The problem was not solved until the Australian Government Minister with responsibility for Cocos, the Rt Hon. Sir Paul Hasluck, visited the islands on two occasions and arranged for 150 Cocos Malay people to be transferred to Christmas Island in 1957–58.

During the 1950s the Malay *kampong* was gradually rebuilt along different lines from the war-time layout. New houses were constructed from precast concrete, although the basic floorplan remained the same as the old *atap* (palm-thatched) buildings.

The estate was fortunate to pick up some lucrative government contract work on West and Direction Islands. The workers themselves saw little increase in their plastic token wages, however, and could only spend them in the Clunies-Ross Store on Home Island.

Opportunities for interaction with mainland Australians were mainly restricted to work contacts on West Island and these suffered badly from the language barrier. Home Island education was as basic and as limited as it had always been. No West Islander knew very much about the other side of the lagoon, as entry to Home Island was by invitation only. Secret liaisons were arranged, nevertheless, for the exchange of fruit and consumer goods for fresh fish and craft-work. The Malay partners in these exchanges risked punishment by fines and unpaid work if they were reported to the estate's *Imarat* (Council of Headmen). Cleverly, the traders adopted pseudonyms so that their identity remained a secret. Clandestine trading like this was carried on in the coconut groves of Cocos for almost 30 years!

The Australian Government mounted a number of health surveys of Home Island, their main focus being on the endemic hookworm and its associated anaemia and debility. The total lack of any toilet facilities in the Malay community exacerbated the problem and consequently it persisted right up until the government-sponsored sewerage scheme began in the mid-1980s.

Three cyclones brushed the territory in the 1950s, each causing a degree of damage to the plantation. Coconut palm replanting, however, was progressing steadily and the copra production remained stable. The major problem of the time was the Rhinoceros Beetle (*Oryctes rhinocerus*) and bounties were introduced on both the adult and larval stages to try to curb their numbers.

Indonesia's *Konfrontasi* politics and the Australian Government's own preoccupation with its territories of Papua and New Guinea kept the spotlight well away from the Cocos Malay community during most of the 1960s. On West

Island military aircraft movements increased markedly, to the point where they surpassed commercial ones, as Indonesia declared its airspace 'out of bounds'. Thousands of transit aircraft passengers on the Australia to South Africa route arrived and left Cocos without any idea of the conditions under which Cocos Malay Australians were living across the lagoon.

Cocos was battered by the elements almost every year in the 1960s, the climax coming in January 1968 with Cyclone Doreen. The eye of this intense system passed right over the atoll. Buildings were extensively damaged, telephone and power services disrupted and many trees were uprooted. In all, 75 000 coconut palms were lost and the total damage bill was estimated to be $A2 million. Fortunately, no lives were lost.

The 1960s saw the introduction of one particularly modern innovation into the Clunies-Ross Estate, the contraceptive pill. Centralised daily distribution and associated inducements saw to it that this method of population control was almost immediately effective.

Participatory government, the human rights of free movement and open expression, the conventions of the International Labour Organisation and access to hard currency were all denied to the Malay people throughout this time. They also had to suffer the appointment of yet another bitterly despised estate manager who delighted in enforcing the estate's rules as strictly as possible.

In an internal memo in 1968, the Australian Government's official representative on Cocos wrote, "there can be no doubt that such government of the Cocos Islanders as does exist is entirely in the hands of an expatriate English businessman and his transient estate managers." Unfortunately, no one seemed to want to listen to any criticism of the supposedly 'idyllic' lifestyle of the Malay people on Cocos.

The wider world remained blissfully unaware of this feudalistic regime until 1971, when a senior official in the Department of External Territories came to Cocos to see conditions for himself. His consequent report set the presses running and the politicians arguing. He spoke boldly of the lack of mainland-standard education, of restrictions on movements, token coinage redeemable only at the company store, and the lack of lavatories and running water.

The report was widely circulated and debate raged in the media about 'slavery' and 'plastic money'. Word finally reached the United Nations and Australia invited a UN delegation to visit the territory. This they did in August 1974 and their report made heavy reading for both John Clunies-Ross and the Australian Government. Labor Prime Minister

Whitlam commented, ''There is no part of the world where things have changed so little.'' His government drew up a series of reforms that were eventually picked up by the subsequent Liberal Government.

Unfortunately, the political see-sawing that occurred in Australia in the mid-1970s had significant social repercussions on Cocos. The reform package that Whitlam had promised to the Cocos Malay people did not come quickly enough for those who had openly declared their true feelings. The 1975 change of government promised only further delays. Many families left the territory in the face of the social disruption that developed. They moved to Geraldton, Port Hedland and Katanning in Western Australia. From a total of 520 persons in 1974, the Home Island population fell to a mere 253 in 1979.

John Cecil Clunies-Ross during 1974 visit by a United Nations delegation
(*Courtesy United Nations*)

In 1978 the Australian Government negotiated the purchase of the islands from John Clunies-Ross for $A6.25 million. This excluded the five-hectare area on Home Island that comprised his family home. In 1979 a local council was established and a workers' cooperative was set up in the same year to look after the Malay community's business interests.

By the time the political upheavals were over on both the mainland and on Cocos, the Australian Government found itself 'calling home' Cocos families from Singapore, Sabah and the Australian mainland to help provide a sufficient labour force to maintain the plantation and basic services.

Government initiatives in the 1980s saw the introduction of several long-overdue changes on Home Island. At last such things as compulsory education, a safe fresh water supply, sewerage, free elections and the right to decide the islands' future were made available to the Cocos Malay people.

A United Nations mission observed an Act of Self Determination on 6 April 1984 among

Parson bin Yapat, Chairman of the Cocos (Keeling) Islands Council, addresses the United Nations General Assembly, 7 November, 1984. Behind him (left to right) are Cree bin Haig and Wahin bin Bynie. *(Courtesy United Nations videotape)*

the citizens of Home Island. Despite many attempts to divert their attention, the Cocos Malay people voted overwhelmingly in favour of political, social and economic integration with Australia. Soon afterwards most of the land was vested in the Cocos (Keeling) Islands Council and the Australian Government promised to raise the living standards of the Cocos Malay community to mainland equivalents within the decade.

In 1987 the Cocos copra industry was finally declared to be unprofitable, and the islanders are now looking to diversify their limited economic base. No matter what road the Cocos Malay people choose to follow into the future, it is certain that it will be one that they have chosen for themselves. The future belongs to them.

HALUAN PIGIMANA MEMILIH DI DALAM TIGA BAHAGIAN:

ADA TIGA BAHAGIAN

SABAN ORANG HARUS PILIH SATU SAJA (DI ANTARA KE TIGA BAHAGIAN ITU)

KASI TARUH STEMNYA DI DALAM KOTAK YANG ADA DI BAWAH BAHAGIAN YANG ORANG MAHU PILIH

PULU COCOS (KEELING)
COCOS (KEELING) ISLANDS

REFERENDUM (SELF DETERMINATION) ORDINANCE 1984

KERTAS LEKSEN
BALLOT PAPER

DIRECTIONS:

THERE ARE THREE PROPOSALS

YOU ONLY HAVE TO MAKE ONE CHOICE

PLACE YOUR VOTING STAMP IN THE SPACE BELOW THE PROPOSAL YOU PREFER

MERDEKA
INDEPENDENCE

PERSATUAN SAMA AUSTRALIA
INTEGRATION WITH AUSTRALIA

BERSOBAT BEBAS SAMA AUSTRALIA
FREE ASSOCIATION WITH AUSTRALIA

HALUAN PIGIMANA KERTAS KERTAS LEKSEN AKAN DIKERJAKANNYA: SELEPAS KASI SUARA ORANG HARUS KASI LIPAT KERTAS LEKSEN BIAR ORANG LAIN TAK BOLEH TAHU PIGIMANA ORANG PUNYA PILIHAN KASI LIHAT KERTAS LEKSEN ITU SAMA KETUA LEKSEN BIAR IA BOLEH LIHAT 11 MPAT IA SAIN DI BELAKANG KERTAS TERSEBUT KASI MASUK KERTAS LEKSEN ITU KE DALAM LEKSEN PUNYA PETI

DIRECTIONS: FOLD THE BALLOT PAPER SO THAT NOBODY CAN SEE HOW YOU HAVE VOTED SHOW THE PRESIDING OFFICER HIS INITIALS ON THE BACK OF THE BALLOT PAPER PUT THE BALLOT PAPER IN THE BALLOT BOX

"And real money, too — not that phony plastic rubbish!"

Above: Cartoon comment on the
sale of the islands (*Courtesy* The
West Australian, *4 April*, 1978)

Left: Ballot paper used in 1984
Act of Self Determination,
designed especially for non-
literate voters (*Courtesy
Australian Electoral Commission*)

The Cocos Malay People

4

Biar mati anak — Jangan mati adat.
(Better that a child, rather than customs, should die.)

Malay proverb

Few groups of people in the world today are as little known or understood as the Cocos Malay inhabitants of the Cocos (Keeling) Islands. Theirs has been a world sealed off from the outside by geography, history, politics and language. Few outsiders have lived among them and very little has been recorded of their cultural practices and traditions — either now or in the past.

This tiny society has been held together for eight generations by its very isolation, shared economic endeavour, strong family loyalty, a deepening commitment to Islam and a unique version of the old 'trading Malay' language of the East Indies.

Despite their disparate origins, the Cocos Malay people achieved an identity of their own within one generation of settlement on these islands. The 'Cocos-born', as they were officially referred to, lived separately from both the Javanese contract labourers and the European owner-settlers. The Cocos Islanders had their own mosques, their own leaders and their own ceremonies.

The steady turnover of contracted labour from Java refreshed and revitalised the islanders' cultural practices. The early criminal element of this group was in no way its dominant feature. Many learned settlers found their way to Cocos under this arrangement. Among their number were musicians, dancers, story-tellers, craftsmen and religious teachers. Their influence on the 'Cocos-born', from their introduction in the 1880s through until the 1930s, has been highly significant.

Elements of English-Scottish traditions have also been absorbed into Cocos Malay cultural practices. Certain foods, dances and musical influences have a decidedly western flavour. This is especially obvious during the New Year's Eve celebrations (31 December). On this occasion Scottish reels are danced with

Cocos Malay children wearing
traditional island costume and
dancing Scottish reels

great enthusiasm by Cocos Malay people wearing traditional island attire — to the accompaniment of Malay drums and violins.

Today the cornerstone of Cocos Malay society and the focus of each individual's life is the Islamic religion. The Cocos people have been described as 'Islamic' since the days of the first settlement. Their religious knowledge and practices have grown under the influence of the contracted Javanese labourers. Recent contacts with 'long-lost' relatives on Christmas Island, Australia, Malaysia and Singapore have given further impetus to the islanders' religious identity.

THE INFLUENCE OF ISLAM

The influence of Islam is all-pervasive in the lives of its adherents. The Cocos Malay people are devout followers of their religion and few depart from its teachings or observances.

The practice of Islam involves subscribing to a set routine for each day, month and year of one's life. Prayers are said five times daily — at first light, midday, late afternoon, twilight and after dark. These prayers and their timings provide an orderly pattern to every waking day. Bathing, cooking, eating and working are all integrated around prayer times.

Each month of the Islamic calendar has a special focus and its own set of observances. The first day of the first month commemorates the time when the prophet left Mecca to start the first Islamic community in Medina in 622 AD. The twelfth day of the third month is *Maulud Nabi*, the prophet's birthday. The 27th day of the seventh month recalls the prophet's ascension from the ruins of a temple in Jerusalem. The eighth month, known on Cocos as *Bulan Arwah*, is a time of remembrance of the deceased relatives in each family. It is marked by large gatherings every three or four days at houses representing each of the broad family groupings in the *kampong*. The ninth month is *Bulan Puasa* (Ramadan), the fasting month, when adult Muslims will not eat or drink during daylight hours. The first day of the tenth month is the celebration of *Hari Raya Puasa* (or *Lebaran*), the festival of the breaking of the fast. The tenth day of the twelfth month is *Hari Raya Haji*, the high point of the month of pilgrimage to Mecca.

The Islamic calendar is based on a lunar rather than a solar year. It is 354 days in length and bears no relation to the four seasons. As each 'month' depends on the actual sighting of the moon for confirmation, precision in long-range forecasting is difficult in a small, isolated place like Cocos. A further complication lies in the fact that a Muslim day begins at sunset, whereas a Western calendar day is reckoned from midnight. Friday night is therefore referred to as 'the eve of Saturday'.

The Cocos community has three mosques, each with an *imam* (priest) and a number of deputy imams. These priests are not full-time clergy. Each has a regular job as well as his commitment to the mosque.

If possible, each set of prayers should be offered in the mosque itself. Failing this, people elect to pray in a designated part of their home or workplace. As a consequence, it is considered respectful to remove one's shoes before entering a Malay household, as the home is also a centre of prayer.

Cocos Malay Muslims are particularly strict in matters of food and drink. Like Islamic people anywhere, they will not consume pork products. As well as this, they are particularly strict about all animals being *halal*-killed. This means that they must be slaughtered according to the correct Islamic rite. Islam teaches that no animal should be killed at all, unless it is needed for human consumption. All taking of animal life therefore requires a prayer to be spoken.

In keeping with most Middle Eastern and Asian people, Cocos Islanders will use only their right hand for eating, giving and receiving. The left hand is reserved for ablutions. Most Cocos Malay people reject alcohol in all its forms. Dogs are regarded as unclean animals and people who are licked by one must ritually cleanse themselves seven times with sand and water.

Arrival at another's house is always announced by the Arabic phrase, *Assalamu alaikum!* (I come in peace), and is answered by the occupants with *Wa'alaikum salam* (Peace be with you). Unless the front door of a house is wide open, it is considered more polite to go around to the back door than to knock on the front.

Cocos Malay children study the *Koran* every afternoon

FROM BIRTH TO ADULTHOOD

The first words that are whispered in a new-born baby's ear comprise the Islamic call-to-prayer, *Allahu Akbar* (God is great). The newly-born are believed to be especially vulnerable to malevolent influences. A coconut oil lamp is kept burning constantly during a child's first week of life, and for three days the baby's placenta is kept under his or her bed. It is placed in a clam shell and mixed with salt, ash and a nail and is covered. It is the father's duty to dispose of this 'guardian' from a *jukong* (sailing boat) into a swift-moving section of the lagoon. He releases it slowly and gently into the water with his right hand — to guard against the religious awkwardness of the child's becoming left-handed. A small swish broom made from coconut fronds is also kept beside each new-born infant. Beneath the baby's pillow the mother will place a comb, a mirror and a pair of scissors. All of these precautions are taken against the possibility of malevolent forces.

A blessing ceremony is held approximately seven days after a birth to mark the child's successful passage through this 'danger period'. The actual timing of this celebration will vary from child to child, as it relies upon the withering of the tied-off umbilical cord. Local superstition holds that the longer the wait, the naughtier the child will be! This 'seventh day' ceremony also serves to bestow the child's name. Until quite recently the infant mortality rate has been remarkably high among these people, so these customs are very strongly adhered to.

Unless 40 days have passed, the child and mother are not permitted to go outside their house, and the child's feet are not allowed to touch the ground. This time is marked by another ceremony at which the baby's hair is cut, rosewater sprinkled on the brow and baby girls' ears pierced. For the next two or three months the mother will always carry a straw from the baby's swish broom with her if she takes her child away from the immediate vicinity of their house at night. Most Cocos Malay fathers make a wooden cradle for their

youngsters and this swings from the ceiling in a breezy part of the house. Inside the cradle, the child's first pillow and a small straw broom accompany the baby.

Should a new-born child display any kind of deformity, this will usually be attributed to some inappropriate parental behaviour during pregnancy. Twins are separated from each other with one being adopted out. Mothers

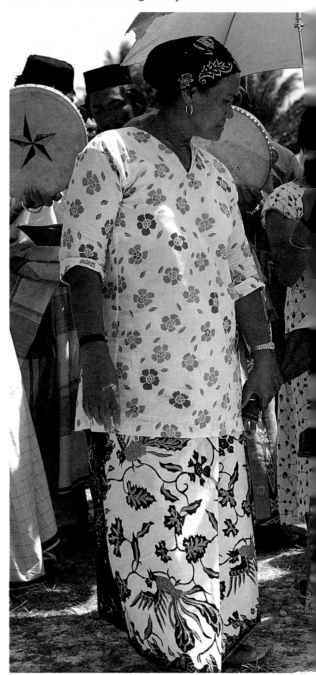

who experience difficulty breast feeding quickly find a relative to wet-nurse their baby. Couples unable to have a baby may even be given a child by relatives. Sickly children are likely to undergo a change of name in an effort to repel any evil influences.

Circumcision takes place on Cocos when boys are five or six years old, in keeping with the islanders' perception of Islamic custom.

Cocos Malay boys dressed as bridegrooms, prior to their circumcision ceremony

In the past this was a time of great celebration for the families of the boys concerned. The lad would be dressed and paraded through the *kampong* just like a bridegroom. Sometimes a boy would accompany a bridal couple on their ceremonial walk. A circumcision feast would then be held and a shadow-puppet, traditional drama or a special dance performance would follow (see page 85). This stylish dance, performed by a line of kneeling men, is known as the *Rodat*. The families of boys of similar ages might combine their celebrations at this time, or a family with a number of boys might arrange for them all to be circumcised together. Traditionally, the operation was conducted by a person known as a *bengkong*, using a bamboo knife at about six o'clock in the morning. Today these operations are performed in the Cocos hospital and the associated celebrations are far less elaborate.

All Cocos Malay children commence religious training soon after circumcision. Daily classes are held in several houses and in the mosques. The youngsters learn to read and write *Jawi*, the Arabic script in which the Koran is written. These classes continue until the students read aloud with ease any page of the Koran. At the age of 14 or 15 a *Menghaji* ceremony is held in which the young girl or boy reads aloud various passages from the Koran. If they complete this task without error before an audience of their religious elders, they are accepted as adults within the mosque.

At approximately the same age, a small ceremony may also be arranged for a number of young people to have their upper front teeth filed straight across. This custom is said to echo a passage in the prophet Muhammad's life where he filed his teeth straight after they were hit by a stone that was dropped into a well where he was hiding.

Courtship is not encouraged until the young people are considered to be 'old enough'. In times past either the estate manager or the headmen would physically punish those considered too young who had liaisons with the opposite sex. A young man displays his interest in a girl by giving her family gifts of fish, fruit, coconuts and other items of food. They may then meet at one or the other's house, or at that of a close relative. There they must be chaperoned and return home at a reasonable hour. Once the relationship has the agreement of both sets of parents, the couple begin to be seen together publicly and are described as being 'engaged'. It is not considered good form for a young man or woman to have had too many suitors.

Unfortunately for the young people concerned, the small population of the islands does not give them a great deal of choice in marriage partners. Strict safeguards are maintained to ensure that people do not marry any of their own relatives. Village interrelationships are well known to all and people grow up in the knowledge of just who their eligible partners are. Marriages are regarded as tangible economic and social links between families. If parents do not approve of a particular liaison, they will act to terminate it. If two families are already linked by a marriage, then no further marital links are encouraged between them. Generally speaking, it is considered desirable that the oldest child marries before any younger brothers and sisters.

Young people with a physical handicap may have a marriage partner organised for them from Singapore or Malaysia. An unmarried person of eligible age is considered unusual and considerable pressure is exerted on him or her to conform to community expectations.

MARRIAGE

A significant rise in community status occurs upon marriage and a further elevation follows the birth of children.

Cocos weddings are huge events that involve almost everyone in the community. No marriages are permitted during the second month of the Islamic calendar (*Safar*), the ninth month (*Ramadan*) or the first part of the month of pilgrimage. Popular times are the first month (*Muharram*), the seventh month (*Rajab*) and the tenth month (*Shawwal*). If it fits into this pattern, the Australian Christmas-New Year holiday period is also a favourite time. Many islander families plan their vacations around the wedding of a relative on Cocos or the mainland. Recently, a few have even travelled to Singapore to witness a relative's marriage.

A wedding on Cocos spans three weeks. A fortnight before the marriage a *Melamar* ceremony is held in the bride's house. Here the groom's father formally requests the girl's hand for his son, often in quite poetic terms. He then presents her family with a number of sarong-wrapped bundles of personal items. These are 'inspected' by the *imam* and counted out for all those gathered to see and hear. The gifts are mainly sarongs, material, jewellery, perfume and money. A humorous item, such as a child's toy, might be hidden in the bundles to amuse those gathered on these relatively informal occasions.

One week before the wedding most of the menfolk gather at the houses of the two families and erect a *tarop*, or overhead shelter, at the front of each. The two houses then become popular gathering places for friends and relatives. During the following week the bride and groom are kept inside their own homes, and their faces, arms and legs are regularly daubed with a yellow paste known as *lulur*. This is believed to progressively soften and lighten their skin. More and more relatives come to stay at the two houses. Every meal is now communal and the number of guests gradually increases as the week goes on. On the Thursday night in each house a *pajangan* or *pelamin* (throne or platform) is constructed and decorated. The couple meet briefly on the Friday morning, after the *imam* has bathed them and go to the graveyard together to pay their respects to their ancestors.

The marriage bond is tied in a religious sense on the Friday night when the Islamic *Nika* ceremony is held for the groom in the mosque. The fathers of the couple are questioned by the *imam* and the groom makes a promise before the gathered elders that he is quite sincere about the step he is about to take. The groom's father then presents the *mas*

kahwin (wedding jewellery) to the *imam* for his inspection.

Legally, the couple are married on the Saturday morning when they proceed together to the Council Chambers and sign the register. The luncheons that follow at the two houses are the biggest meals of the fortnight, and every member of the Malay community and many West Island friends are invited.

Mid-afternoon sees the public affirmation of the wedding. The groom leads a procession of chanting relatives to the girl's home. In his belt he wears the traditional Malay dagger known as a *kris*. This ancient Malay status symbol is said to possess great mystical powers on ceremonial occasions such as this. As the groom's party reaches the bride's house, one of his attendants forces his entry. Inside the house the couple are finally linked in an emotional, symbolic series of gestures by the bride's mother. Soon afterwards the couple emerge and walk together in procession.

Over:
Cocos Malay wedding procession

On their return they are honoured by several performers of *silat pengantin*, a symbolic martial art in which the performers assume a trance state and utilise the psychic power they gain from touching the bridal couple. The bride and groom then sit as 'king and queen' for the day on the throne prepared for them. Religious blessings are said for them and large quantities of food are brought forward to be blessed in their company. This is then distributed to all who helped to make the day a success.

Several nights of dancing follow, the most important being the *Melenggok*, or scarf dance, usually performed by men. This is accompanied by several smaller, and highly emotional, ceremonies in which the couple are accepted into their new families. Any old animosities between the two groups are openly aired and settled. The couple will then take up residence in one of the two households. There are no hard and fast rules governing which one — it is usually a matter of convenience.

PARENTHOOD AND MALAY NAMES

Cocos Malay people are given just one name when they are born. This is followed by *bin* (son of) or *binte* (daughter of) preceding their father's only name. For example, Abdul bin Hanif is the son of Hanif. Asmi binte Hanif is Hanif's daughter. These given names are not changed on marriage. This can cause a little confusion when people travel to the mainland.

In the example just given, Hanif's son would prefer to be called, 'Mr Abdul' and his wife, 'Mrs Abdul' in a Western situation. The title of 'Mr Hanif' really belongs to Abdul's father.

After their first child is born, a Cocos Malay couple are respectfully referred to as '*Mak*' or '*Pak*' together with the name of this baby. For example, after the birth of a child named Abdul, his parents will become known in the community as '*Mak* and *Pak* Abdul'. It would be disrespectful to refer to them by their childhood names any longer. These are only retained for legal purposes.

This name change signifies a change of status in the community and occurs regardless of the sex of the child. Similarly, upon the birth of the first grandchild, another change of name and status occurs. If *Mak* and *Pak* Abdul's first grandchild is called Fatima, they both become '*Nek* Fatima' (see Appendix).

Young parents are greatly assisted by the presence of grandparents in the same household. This allows them to adjust to their new roles slowly, under the expert guidance of their own parents and relatives. In this way, the customs associated with pregnancy, birth and infancy are easily passed from one generation to the next. There is never any shortage of willing baby-sitters to look after the youngster, either.

Malay children grow up in a very comfortable social environment. There is always someone to minister to their needs. Crying babies are never uncomfortable for long. They become accustomed to a wide range of people picking them up and entertaining them. They are always the centre of attention. Theirs is a very safe and predictable social and physical world.

Correct social behaviour is quickly learned by island youngsters. It is not polite to walk in front of someone if you can walk behind them. If you pass in front of others, you must stoop slightly to show respect. Eat, give and receive with your right hand only. Never point at people; gesture with your head instead. In adult company you should wait until you are spoken to.

Melenggok dancing on the wedding night

OLD AGE AND DEATH

Elders and heads of families are accorded great respect in the Cocos Malay community and it is the duty of the youngest child to take direct responsibility for his or her ageing parents.

Old people contribute in many ways to the young family in whose house they live. They provide religious and social guidance and they also contribute in a material sense by fishing, cooking or child-minding. No social pressure is placed on them and they live life at their own pace. If they become ill, the lady of the household will look after them closely.

When a death occurs in the Cocos Malay community, all work ceases and people immediately take steps to organise the burial. The deceased is washed, dressed and laid out

accompanies the grieving family to the grave yard. Four people carry the litter and a fifth holds a small white sunshade made with bamboo sticks over the top.

The body is slowly lowered into its deep, north-south oriented grave. The person is laid full-length on their side in an area dug out to one side of the base of the shaft of the grave. They lie with their head pointing northwards and their face to the western wall. The body is held in place with pumice stones and the entrance to this small cavern within the grave is sealed with wooden planking. The grave-shaft is filled in with sand and a small wooden or concrete rectangle placed on top. At its head and foot a *mesan* or funerary post is erected, the shape of which indicates the sex of the deceased. The person's name will then be carved in *Jawi* (Arabic letters) into the wood or soft cement of the *mesan*. The funerary sun-shade, stretcher and a few personal possessions will be left beside the grave. Some of the white cloth will be torn into short strips for mourners to tie around their right wrists. It is believed that as the material slowly withers and falls away, so too will the wearer's grief.

Mourning ceremonies continue in the deceased's house for seven days after the death. The family then keep a daily tally and organise further memorial ceremonies after 40 and 100 days. Two annual death-anniversaries are then observed and the final remembrance ceremony is held after 1000 days. It is not considered polite to refer directly to a recent death. Even later, as in English, a person is not usually described as being 'dead' (*mati*), but rather as having 'passed away' (*meninggal*).

in the house for a short time for people to pay their last respects. Many blessings are said and flowers are scattered over the body. The deceased is then wrapped in nine white cloths and placed on a specially made bamboo stretcher with the arching stems of palm fronds forming a cover. The entire litter is then covered in colourful sarongs. A procession

FAMILY CEREMONIES

Throughout the year a large number of *selamatan* (blessing) ceremonies are held at various houses in the *kampong* for a wide range of small family celebrations. These include name-giving, house-blessing, welcomes, farewells, boat-launchings, remembrances of deceased relatives, circumcisions and other family events worthy of a religious blessing. An individual's birthday is not a big event and their occasional celebration is a relatively recent development.

When a *selamatan* ceremony is held, the lounge room of the house will be cleared of furniture and a large sheet of material laid out to cover the floor. The family's *imam* and his mosque's committee members will arrive in prayer attire and sit cross-legged around the edges of the room. The *imam* will then make the appropriate blessings as he burns frankincense in a small chalice. Food will be laid out in the centre of the room and later distributed to all who take part. Usually the head of the household makes a speech about the particular occasion and cites the names of many friends and relatives whom he would like to include in the current blessing. These are all-male events with the female relatives remaining very much in the background.

A meal may then be offered to the mosque committee and other invited guests. This will be spread out on long trestles from which people will serve themselves after a formal request to commence eating. Drinks are served to the guests by young friends and relatives of the household.

FASTING AND THE HARI RAYA FESTIVAL

The biggest celebration of the year for the Cocos Malay community is *Lebaran* or *Hari Raya Puasa*, the day that marks the end of the Islamic fasting month of Ramadan. The fast is held during the ninth month on the Muslim calendar, remembering the time during which the Muslim holy-book, the Koran, was first revealed to Muhammad. As the Islamic calendar is ten or eleven days shorter than the Christian calendar, the fasting month occurs a little earlier each year. Indeed, over thirty-two and a half years, it moves right through the Christian calendar and every season.

As the time draws near to commence fasting, a close watch is kept on the moon. When it is new and only just visible the fast begins. Often the *imams* and members of their committees will commence a day before their congregations, so as to finish with time to organise community celebrations.

Islamic fasting involves no eating, drinking, smoking or sexual activity during daylight hours. Children over seven are encouraged to fast for a part of each day, and increase their observance as they grow older. Fasting is not obligatory for the sick or the very old. Those women who are pregnant, breastfeeding or menstruating are not permitted to fast. Exemptions may also be granted to soldiers and travellers, but any days lost by indisposition should be made up later.

Islamic adherents believe that the self-control learned by fasting helps them to learn to curb bodily desires and self-indulgence. It also creates an awareness of the plight of the poor and acts as a stimulus to charity. As all Islamic people in the world are fasting together during Ramadan the experience helps to reinforce a strong feeling of belonging to a wider community.

Cocos Malay people begin fasting around five o'clock in the morning and cease soon after six o'clock at night. Every night in the mosque a chapter of the Koran is read aloud before the normal prayers. These regular prayers are then repeated 23 consecutive times. Most men and many women make an effort to attend the mosque during this month, rather than praying at home.

The mosques' drums are beaten every night of the fasting month

On the sixteenth night a celebration known as *Malam Ketupat* is held. This is the night of the full moon. Two types of *ketupat* are cooked and prepared for this night. They are both sweet rice-cakes cooked inside woven palm-leaf packets. These are always served cut in half, symbolising the half-way point in the month. On the 21st night *Malam Pasong* is celebrated. The delicacy for this night, *kueh pasong*, is only made on this one day of the year. It is a sweet and glutinous mixture served in a cone-shaped banana-leaf wrapper, the shape of which symbolises the 'narrowing down' of the month. After this night, lights are placed outside every house and people go to their family's *imam* to deliver their alms or *Zakat Fitra*. This is a quantity of rice which varies with the size of each family. On the 29th day the *imams* complete their fast and are busy ritually killing any chickens that will form part of the next day's celebrations.

The last day arrives and a *Sedekah* ceremony is held at each of the three *imam's* houses, utilising the donated rice. From here the *imams* and deputy *imams* proceed to every household in their congregation and conduct a special kind of ceremony known as a *Kondangan*. During these occasions the head of each household welcomes the official party to his house and recites all the names of his family and relatives whom he would like to have included in the blessing. A lot of food is prepared, laid out, blessed and distributed from each home. These ceremonies take up the entire afternoon.

When night falls, there is a sharp rise in excitement as *Hari Raya* has now commenced. This first night of the new month is known as *Malam Terkeber*. The final chapter of the Koran is read, sermons are given, the year is reviewed, votes of thanks are offered, gifts to the mosque are presented and the fast is officially declared over. Drum-beating and chanting then continue non-stop until dawn. People dress up, walk around the *kampong* and visit their friends' houses all night long. Morning prayers are said and then follow some very emotional outpourings as each member of the congregation greets and begs forgiveness from every other member for any misunderstandings or personal oversights during the past year. Visits are then

A *Kondangan* ceremony, the afternoon before *Hari Raya*

Hari Raya morning — a highly emotional end to a night's chanting as each person begs forgiveness

made to the other mosques and similar emotional exchanges occur there.

Soon after dawn the entire community walks to the cemetery, where graves are tidied, and prayers and offerings are made for every known ancestor. Those whose graves have been lost in the ravages of time are not forgotten, as prayers and offerings are made for them at the water's edge.

Back in the *kampong*, huge lunches are then prepared for the many friends and relatives who have been invited to each house. Many people find themselves with a number of luncheon invitations and endeavour to eat a little at each place. Gifts are exchanged and the young children really enjoy themselves.

All Cocos families enjoy a week's holiday from work at this time. Sailing and sporting competitions with generous prizes are organised every day and a big night of

dancing is usually arranged. It is a most joyous and indulgent week of celebrating. Nowadays this has become a very popular time of year for mainland relatives to visit Cocos and many 'long-lost' friendships are rekindled.

OTHER FESTIVALS

There are two other big days on the Cocos religious calendar: *Hari Raya Haji* and *Hari Maulud Nabi*.

Hari Raya Haji is the tenth day of the twelfth Islamic month: the time of the pilgrimage to Mecca. All Muslims hope to visit this holiest of cities at some time in their lives. In 1986 the first-ever Cocos contingent of three couples made an historic journey to Saudi Arabia to fulfil this vow. On this day each year special commemorative prayers are held in the mosques in the morning.

Jukongs are readied
for a week's racing
at *Hari Raya* time

Hara Raya week is packed with sports and novelty competitions

Watching the fun during *Hari Raya* week

Hari Maulud Nabi, the birthday of the Prophet Muhammad, is the twelfth day of the third Islamic month. The mosques are beautifully decorated and a small procession is often arranged in which groups of chanting people walk through the community behind a banner bearing ornate, Arabic-written prayers.

THE SPIRIT WORLD

As the Cocos Malay people have come more and more under the influence of Islam, their experience and awareness of a spirit world has begun to diminish. There are still many individuals, however, who acknowledge and are fearful of supernatural forces. As with Malay people elsewhere, there is a belief in a soul substance or vital force (*semangat*) possessed by all things in the universe, whether alive, dead, animate or inanimate. Each person's head is the focus of his or her *semangat*, so it is socially inappropriate to place one's hand on any Malay person's head.

87

Every house has a guardian spirit that protects it. Every major natural feature or large tree has a similar *penunggu* (guardian). As well as these protective forces, the Home Islanders also acknowledge the presence of evil. Some people will wear a small cotton sachet containing prayers, frankincense and other fragrant substances around their neck to ward off evil influence. Newly-cut hair and finger nails are often buried or burned to prevent anyone using them to invoke the forces of evil against the owner.

A person who disappears or who dies without the Islamic *air jalan* (last rites) is not

Raden Jayadrata

Bambang Aswatama

Two shadow puppet characters used in traditional Cocos Malay drama
(*Courtesy Cocos Museum*)

believed to be properly at rest. These lost souls (*siluman*) are thought to wander around and are occasionally spotted by members of the community. They are ragged people who do not mean any harm. There are some other spirit-characters who are decidedly evil, however, and a person who sights one of these may have convulsions and require a ritual cleansing. Dark places, night-time and situations in which people are on their own lend themselves to spirit sightings. For this reason, Malay people will always take a bush-knife (*parang*) with them when they go to uninhabited islands. Few people like to venture outside after dark and several households sleep with their lights on. People are never keen to work on their own, particularly at night. Few ever go anywhere near the cemetery at non-ceremonial times.

Certain individuals are said to have power over the spirit world. Such people are called *dukuns*. Some have control over evil forces, some over the forces against evil. If people believe that they are under an evil influence, or have found evidence to suggest that someone is trying to weaken them, they will seek assistance from a *dukun*. Those capable of invoking evil, claim to have made people fall ill, or to have produced odd aches and pains in the back or stomach of their victim. As well as the faith healers and evil-doers there are also *dukuns* who are clairvoyants, midwives, *bengkongs* (circumcision performers) and others who are capable of 'good magic'.

The pantheon of spirit-characters acknowledged by the Cocos Malay people is very similar to that of the wider Malay world. There are ghost hags, goblins, a head with trailing viscera, a wish-granting coconut and a talking tree. Spirit-possession usually follows some sudden shock or surprise which develops into a form of hysteria. Hysteric blindness, abrupt changes of voice, the uttering of meaningless gibberish and ghastly visions of dead people may all occur. In recent times, however, these events have been much less frequent on Cocos — a fact that the people themselves attribute to the strengthening of Islam.

THE COCOS MALAY LANGUAGE

The Malay dialect spoken by the Cocos Malay people is an unsophisticated, oral language. It contains words that reflect the diverse origins of these people and their history of sporadic contacts with outsiders. Many words and turns of phrase reflect turn-of-the-century trading Malay, swear words hail from a wide range of islands in the East Indies and technical words echo a close contact with English-speaking overseers.

Little schooling occurred in the days of the estate, so few people have had the opportunity to read or write down their mother tongue. There are no records of the ways in which the language might have changed since the days of early settlement. Some of the contracted labourers are remembered as speaking Javanese and being quite difficult to understand. Of necessity, modern interpretation is given in Bahasa Indonesia/Malaysia with some adaptations to local usage.

The intonation pattern of the Cocos Malay language is quite different from that of Indonesian. The letter 'r' is not rolled as heavily and many words are local adaptations of English and Malay words. Pronunciation sometimes varies a little between speakers and little mutual correction occurs. In general conversation words are often abbreviated and sentences are left unfinished. Key words and phrases may be echoed back to the speaker by the listener.

It is interesting to note that in the traditional Malay poems (*pantun*) which have been passed down through the generations, one finds words that are not in everyday use. Many of these poems are about love. Each verse begins with two lines that mainly serve to create a reflective mood. The third and fourth lines deliver the poem's true message and may have a cryptic connection to the first pair. *Pantuns* can still be heard during the nights of *Seylong* dancing in the week following a wedding. Dancers will *pantunkan* (recite or compose these poems) to their partners. Sometimes quite a competition develops.

Kalok ada sumur di ladang
Boleh saya menumpang mandi?
Kalok ada umur panjang
Boleh kita berjumpa lagi.

If there is a well in the field,
May I bathe there?
If we live a long life,
I hope we meet again.

Langit tinggi mana tanggannya?
Pintu sorga mana kuncinya?
Sunting dunia kita berdua
Becerai hidup sakit rasanya.

Lengkuas hidup lengkuas mati
Melati kudup di tengah padan.
Becerai mati puas di hati
Becerai hidup mata memandang.

Kapal Bugis memuat cita
Sudah sarat belenggang lagi.
Habis budi habis cinta
Jangan diharap digendang lagi.

Where are the stairs to the sky?
Where is the key to paradise?
Stay together in this world —
Divorce is too high a price.

The herb lives, the herb dies,
Jasmine blooms in the lane.
To part at death is sadness —
To part in life is shame.

The trading ship brings cloth
So we can dance again.
If love is gone, then honour's gone —
Don't hope to be blessed again.

Jalan-jalan sepanjang jalan
Air di pancor sunyinya dalam.
Dari dipandang baik'an jangan
Bikin ancur hati di dalam.

Strolling slowly down the road —
That fountain has a silence deep.
It's better not to look at it —
For if you do your heart will weep.

FISHING AND FOOD

The two staples of the Cocos Malay diet are fish and rice. Until quite recently fish, and occasionally seabirds and chicken, were the only source of animal protein in the islanders' diet. Despite their modern access to all manner of meat, the Cocos Malay people still consume large quantities of local fish.

The most popular method of fishing is the hand-line (*mancing*), using crabs or shellfish for bait. Fish caught in this manner include parrot-wrasse, sea-perch and snapper. All these fish are taken inside the lagoon in areas with patches of coral surrounded by sand.

Trolling (*menunda*) is employed in the deeper lagoon waters and just outside Port Refuge. Flying fish or metallic spinners are used as bait. A greater element of luck is involved in this type of fishing, but the rewards might include huge sailfish, barracuda or tuna.

Two types of fishing nets are used on the islands, the long seine-net (*jaring*) and the circular casting-net (*jala*). The *jaring* is about two metres high and 40 m long. It has floats along the top and weights along the base. These nets are employed on the southern lagoon tidal flats and are stretched between two boats. Other boats then drive any fish schools towards the net, which quickly encircles them. As the circle closes the fishermen jump into it and catch the entangled fish by hand.

The casting-net is used on the reef-flat and in the lagoon wherever schools of small fish are fairly visible. These little fish often become the bait for larger ones.

Spear throwing (*menumbak*) is also employed on the outer reef with great accuracy. Schools of unsuspecting, large coral-grazing fish are the major targets. Unfortunately, this skill is now declining in the face of the easy availability of high-speed boats and spear-guns.

Crayfish are eagerly sought along the reef at night and large mud-crabs can be taken from the lagoon's mud-flats at low tide. Octopus, squid, clams, a type of turbo shell (*kepala biola*) and the favourite spider-shell (*gong-gong*) are all taken by family groups when the tide is low. Even the puffer-fish, with its deadly poisonous innards, is carefully prepared and eaten with delight.

Most Cocos fish are fried, although some are boiled and some curried. Several varieties of fish *sambal* (piquant sauce) are popular and are made by crushing dried fish and spices with a mortar and pestle.

Rice cannot be grown on Cocos and has always been imported. Even though there is an increasing use of bread in Malay homes, it is still felt that no day should pass without at least one good meal of rice and fish. Frozen, filleted fish are carried to the mainland almost every week by holidaying Cocos Malay people as prized gifts for relatives. The mainlanders, in turn, give their island visitors cases of fresh fruit for their return journey. This modern fruit-for-fish exchange echoes the bartering that occurred up to 1978 between the Home Islanders and the residents of West and Direction Islands. In those days they risked heavy fines from the estate. Today the only penalty is a hefty excess baggage charge!

During most meals the senior men and any guests will eat first. A helping of rice will be served to each of them and they will then add to this themselves from the selection of foods spread before them. Every meal will have some fish, a *sambal* and a choice of other dishes. Cocos Malay people like most of their food to be spiced. Eating is usually done with the fingers of the right hand, carefully ensuring that no food extends beyond the second finger joint.

The women of the household will serve drinks for the diners and will later retire to the kitchen to eat their own meal while their husbands attend to the guests. Large social events may involve three or more sittings. Everyday family meals are much quieter affairs and all members will usually sit together at the one table.

Nowadays, Cocos Malay meals may include a wider range of fruit and vegetables. They are also showing an increasing influence from Malaysia and Singapore. Returnees and relatives have introduced several new items into the Cocos diet, the most popular being fried noodles and sweet-sauced satay sticks. While still being rather conservative eaters, the Cocos Malay people are gradually sampling new dishes and steadily adding to their repertoire.

HOUSING

Housing design has recently changed quite dramatically on Home Island. Families now enjoy dwellings of a high, mainland-equivalent standard with running hot and cold water and electricity. Until as recently as 1983 the Home Island community were without sewerage or a reliable water supply. Solar hot-water systems were introduced in 1987.

Up until the 1950s the houses of the *kampong* had a north-south orientation and were constructed with local building materials. They were built off the ground on top of short stumps. The walls were made from a kind of cane, obtained from the spine of the palm-frond, the frame was made from local hard-wood and the roof from layers of woven palm-fronds. They were roughly square in shape and were partitioned into three areas; one served as a sitting room and two for sleeping.

Mattresses were made from sacking filled with rags and dry grass. Kapok could be bought at the store, but was expensive, so pillows were often stuffed with dried seagrass. In large households people slept in every room, including the kitchen. In keeping with local custom, however, no one to this day will sleep with their head towards the north — as this orientation is reserved for the dead.

These *atap* homes were replaced by east-west oriented concrete houses in the 1950s. Their walls were cast inside huge moulds and their design was similar to the earlier *atap* model. Wooden kitchens, storage sheds and wash-houses were built separately at the back, as before. Water for household use was drawn by hand from backyard wells right up until the 1980s.

The current housing design was developed from the results of extensive surveys of family living patterns and expressions of community desires. The rebuilding programme is being carried out by the islanders themselves, and has been largely financed by the Australian Government as part of a promise to upgrade community services on Home Island to main-land standards.

Housing styles, 1980s
and 1950s

Nek Renja, Cocos identity, walks through the *kampong* on Home Island, 1945. *(Courtesy A. de Groot, U.K.)*

Basket-making from coconut fronds

COCOS MALAY CRAFTS

Craftsmanship in any community revolves around the availability of natural resources. The many products of the coconut palm and the beautiful dark wood of the Ironwood tree are the major raw materials in Cocos crafts. Sadly, this latter species has been savagely cut back over the last 40 years and is increasingly hard to obtain.

In the early years of settlement the Cocos Malay people fashioned dug-out canoes from large local trees (*Hernandia peltata*). They had no outriggers and were mainly used for line fishing in the lagoon. A few had sails, but most were paddled. They were described by lone sailor, Joshua Slocum, who visited these islands in 1897, as 'exquisitely modelled' and displaying the best workmanship he had seen on his voyage. Unfortunately, these craft (*jukong balok*) disappeared from use in the 1920s.

Any small vessel designed for use in Cocos waters has to cope with the peculiar characteristics of the lagoon. It is quite rough and choppy in the centre and north, yet exceedingly shallow towards the south.

The present design of the Malay sailing-boat, the *jukong*, is the end result of several generations of Scottish and Malay adaptations. The bottom is broad and bears a keel of about 150 mm. This permits the craft to lean well over in shallow water and yet have sufficient draft to handle the choppy mid-lagoon waters. There are two basic models of *jukong*: the

The *jukong*, traditional sailing craft

95

straight-sided and the round-sided. They are each constructed in various sizes and are all steered with a rudder and lines. Each has one mast with two sails, a jib and a mainsail. A spinnaker and bowsprit can also be used to great effect when racing.

The majority of these boats were built in the estate workshops by teams of four men working continually for a month on each boat. Much of the wood used was imported from Java. Private individuals could also construct boats in their spare time using local wood, but this could take them up to nine months. Many of the round-sided boats one sees today were privately built. The last *jukong* was built in the late 1970s. Since then, aluminium motor boats have proved more popular with the younger generation. Any small *jukong* spotted out on the lagoon today will probably be under the direction of an old man, catching fish for his children. The larger *jukongs* are dusted off at least once a year — during the week-long *Hari Raya* festivities. Teams of mixed ages and experience sail a difficult course that takes in most of the lagoon as they compete for generous money prizes.

The hard, tightly grained local Ironwood is currently being used to carve ornate angelfish, sharks and model *jukongs* for sale. These intricately carved mementos can command high prices and are eagerly sought by mainlander Australians.

The coconut palm offers a wide choice of raw materials for both the craftsman and the householder. Its fronds can be quickly made into a straight-sided basket for carrying fish. The hard spine of the frond can be peeled and dried and used as cane in conical, round and scoop-shaped baskets. Thicker cane was once used to make the the walls of traditional houses. Freshly cut palm-fronds were used for thatching their roofs. These fronds could also be twisted and bound into rope. The whippy spines of individual fronds are still collected and made into most effective swish brooms. New, soft leaves can be woven into small cube-shapes and filled with rice. The finished product is called a *ketupat*. The embryonic new shoot in the centre of the palm makes a tasty meal. The new flower stalks can be eaten, or they can be bound and cut when still soft to yield a dark, thick sugar. The coconuts themselves provide a coarse husk for fuel, meat for eating or copra production and water for drinking. The inner nut has a hard shell that can be carved and made into ladles and ornaments, or used as fuel. The trunk was once used in construction work and furniture making and the roots, variously treated, made a very effective dye, tobacco and tea. Newly sprouted nuts contain a soft, sweet centre not unlike dried apple and their shoots make a crunchy snack.

Coconut oil can be used to make soap. The oil is boiled in a mixture with the ash of palm-frond stems and well-water. The soapy froth is scooped off and left to harden in flat containers. It will later be cut into cakes. The mixture beneath the froth has cleansing properties as well and is used by menstruating women when they wash their hair. A small amount is also used in the ritual washing of a body before burial.

Tapping the coconut flower for liquid sugar

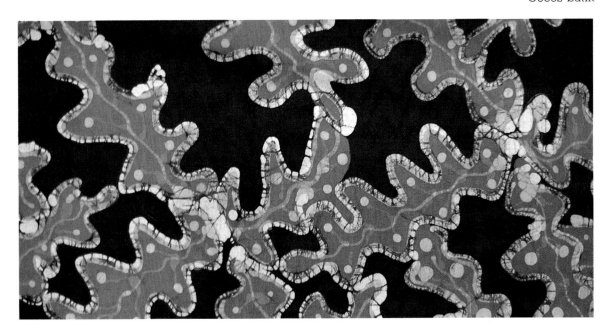

In 1985 the Asian craft of batik was introduced to Cocos. The skills of the workers have since blossomed to the point where Cocos batik is rapidly establishing a reputation in Australia. Their designs and colours cheerfully reflect the islands' environment and sea-life. The islanders are highly skilled carpenters and cabinetmakers and the new houses on Home Island are a lasting tribute to their precise, careful workmanship.

LOCAL GOVERNMENT

Local government in the Territory is in the hands of a seven-member council, elected from among the Home Island community. The council has a wide range of responsibilities on the islands. These include land management, community welfare, conservation, housing, vehicular movements and the provision of basic services.

The community's business interests are looked after by a cooperative society, that has a management board of eight elected by its members. The cooperative controls two shops, a single-workers' mess and hostel, a stevedoring service and a large workforce. The cooperative hostel has recently been upgraded for use by small numbers of tourists.

The members of the cooperative receive a reduced wage, but are spared many community service charges. Each year the society's surplus is distributed to its members in the form of dividends.

Elections to both council and cooperative are conducted by secret ballot using voting papers with photographs of each candidate. Voters, many of whom are illiterate, are asked to place coloured stickers next to the photographs of the people they wish to vote for. The elected committees liaise closely with the Island Administrator on all issues of major importance to the Territory.

Decision-making still takes place in a traditionally Malay fashion. Long discussions are first held in the council chambers and these continue in the homes of neighbours and friends. Here, family elders and women may exert a strong behind-the-scenes influence on the elected decision-makers. Issues are talked over and over until a community consensus is reached as to the preferred course to follow. In recent times community leaders on Cocos have displayed considerable insight and vision as they gradually steer their community towards a more self-reliant, more self-sufficient future on the islands.

WORLD VIEW

The Cocos Malay community is a reserved and self-contained social world. The underlying principle involved in every interpersonal relationship is the continued maintenance of social harmony. As individuals, these people are eager to please and find it hard to ever say 'no'. There is a tendency to tell the outsider what they think he or she might like to hear. Islanders rarely speak directly to a new person or confront someone with whom they have a grievance. This will be done by intermediaries, leaving everyone concerned a degree of room in which to move.

Anger, impatience, strong emotions and loud voices are contained. Personal opinions, no matter how fiercely held, are rarely voiced outside the home. Misfortunes may be blamed on the inappropriate behaviour of others and exceedingly good luck is seen as a reward for strength of faith. Persons who act against the social order may be shunned by the wider community. There is a strong sense of the 'unbecoming' and a huge range of social behaviours are classified as either *enak* or *tak enak* (nice or not nice). Many traditional Cocos ceremonies involve the settling of differences between community members, and present an opportunity to start relations afresh. Deep-seated animosities do not usually thrive for long in such an atmosphere of social reconciliation.

The extended family is the focus of all social life and the standpoint from which all community events are evaluated. Social relationships are characterised by strong family loyalty and an intense bonding to mother-figures. The Cocos Malay egalitarian, Islamic view of society does not permit the growth of many 'tall poppies' and people who display unwarranted ambition or arrogance are usually brought back into line by their peers. A good leader is often a retiring personality who works hard and leads by example rather than authority.

The Cocos Malay people share a common language, religion, heritage, and common customs and feel that they have all that they require within their own society. Few members have ever moved beyond its social borders and fewer still feel any need to do so. Their society is 'closed' inasmuch as any outsider who marries into it must renounce any previous beliefs and undergo conversion to Islam.

Cocos and Christmas Islander communities can be found in Western Australia at Port Hedland, Geraldton, Katanning and Perth. Most of their number find work in the large meatworks in those centres, killing and preparing meat for the Middle Eastern market. Others have obtained jobs with local councils, building companies and government agencies. They are highly respected by fellow Australians as helpful neighbours and good citizens.

Most of these mainland groups are now in close contact with people on Home Island. Annual holidays are often taken with relatives, particularly at wedding or *Hari Raya* times. This increasing contact with more 'mainstream' Malay people has started to have an effect on island customs. Religious observance has become more sophisticated and wedding costumes and practices have fallen more in line with Malaysian styles in recent times.

The Cocos Malay people have shown a remarkable flair for adaptation during their relatively short social history. They have developed the knack of accepting new cultural elements and blending them with traditions of their own. They have also been quick to grasp new technologies and adjust them to local needs.

Despite their inordinately small population, these people have demonstrated that they have the social cohesion necessary to resist being 'swallowed up' by the wider community. In this Australian Bicentennial year we warmly welcome the Cocos Malay people into the mainstream of Australian society and hope that we will be able to learn more about their remote, but unique, community.

Over:
The annual Cocos Olympics provide inter-island fun and competition for all ages

Island Profiles

5

As we ... entered the coral circle the contrast [with the deepest blue ocean depths] was most remarkable. The brilliant colours of the waters, transparent to a depth of over thirty feet, now purple, now of the bluest sky-blue, and now green, with the white crests of the waves flashing under a brilliant sun, the encircling palm-clad islands ... all presented a sight never to be forgotten.

Andrew Leach, on board the *Iphegenia*, reporting to the Colonial Secretary about his arrival at Cocos on 21 July 1897.

HOME ISLAND

Home Island, appropriately named, is the home of the Cocos Malay people. Islanders who have moved away to the Australian mainland or to South-east Asia refer to Home Island as their *tanah air*, their 'well-spring', their homeland. After seven generations of settlement, the Cocos Malay people know no other home and are indeed the products of this unique setting.

This island was the site of the first permanent settlement, that of Alexander Hare, in 1826. It has continued as a well-established community with its own traditional lifestyle.

The island has changed considerably from the early days of settlement when it was known as *Pulu Selma*. Most of the original vegetation has been replaced and marine erosion has altered the coastline in several areas. The most significant changes to the island's coastline, however, have been made by the settlers themselves. The landing area has undergone major reclamation efforts this century. Areas north and south of the present jetty have been built out into the lagoon. The houses now referred to as *Kampong Baru* (new village) were constructed on land reclaimed by teams of village women earlier this century. Sand from two large dunes, countless coral boulders and hundreds of coconut logs were carried by hand and used to fill in a small bay in the area between the present jetty and

Oceania House. The shady avenue of trees along the present waterline was then planted to consolidate the development. The foreshore of the area known as *Kampong Atas* (top village), along the island's southern shore, has been built out and over an old swamp, producing the perfectly straight strand-line we see here today.

Even the present jetty on Home Island is in a relatively new location. For the first 100 years of settlement the main jetty was situated on the south-facing shore near the Clunies-Ross residence, at a point known locally as *Ujung Toko* (storehouse point) or *Gardu* (guardhouse). Visiting ships would follow a dredged channel in to this point. The remains of an old storehouse are still visible on the windy promontory today, although the area appears to have suffered considerable erosion. Narrow-gauged trolley tracks once criss-crossed the main settlement area. These tracks carried small hand-pushed wagons in which the islanders moved cargo to and from the island's stores.

In the period following World War II another major change occured in the natural landscape. The area now known as *Pulu Gangsa*, which serves as the community cemetery, was once a separate island. In the late 1940s it was physically joined onto the northern end of Home Island. Teams of men worked for several weeks to place hundreds of coral rocks and concrete-filled drums across the shallow causeway. These began to catch the drifting sands and the two islands gradually merged into one. Coconuts were planted on the new land and these days it is quite hard to visualise the area as two separate islands. Funeral processions no longer need to transfer to small boats to make this journey to the graveyard. Since the reclamation *Pulu Gangsa* has suffered considerable erosion on its western, lagoon side and many graves have been lost to the ravages of the sea. The remains of an earlier protective wall are still visible about 30 m out into the lagoon.

The community cemetery has not always been at the northern extremity of the island. Last century there were several other grave-sites much closer to the present settlement. The decision to create a separate burial ground was made around the turn of the century after the recommendation of a visiting doctor, who was concerned about the quality of the community's water supply. A couple of these earlier gravesites are still in evidence today. One burial ground was located near the present school. The grave of Suma, an original settler from Alexander Hare's party, can still be seen beneath a tree at the back of the school. Suma arrived on Cocos as a small boy and went on to become an *imam* in the late nineteenth century. His leadership was praised by lone yachtsman, Joshua Slocum, who visited the islands in 1896. Human bones were found in one of the sand-dunes that was levelled in the 1920s during the reclamation work at Kampong Baru. The dune stood where the health centre is now located. Another old burial site was uncovered in 1988 during the construction of the community cyclone shelter.

Wooden jetty and boatsheds, Home Island, 1945 (*Courtesy A. de Groot, U.K.*)

A pair of western-style graves can be found in the area to the south-east of the copra sheds. These belong to a Captain Ballard and his dog. This man and his family lived on Home Island in the mid-nineteenth century, but were struck by tragedy when their two children, Dick and Maria, were lost without trace from the shores of the island now known as *Pulu Maria*.

Tanjong Garam (salty point) was the setting for a gruesome murder in 1912. Two Javanese contracted labourers, Aspin and Sah'it, conspired together to get a third man to join them at this point one night. The innocent Ra'isan had no idea that Aspin was wildly jealous of his being able to be billeted in the house of a pretty young lady named Soda. Aspin was convinced that Ra'isan must have had designs on the girl and was determined to kill him. The devious pair bullied Ra'isan into climbing a tree and then clubbed him down from behind. Aspin drove the sharp end of a piece of wood right through his head. They threw the body into the lagoon off *Tanjong Garam*, not realising that the prevailing current would wash it back up onto the beach the following day. A subsequent post-mortem by the cable station doctor revealed that the assailant was left-handed. A search was conducted, a 'bush court' was convened and Aspin was found guilty of murder. His friend, Sah'it, was found to be his accomplice. The pair were given their last rites and executed by drowning behind Horsburgh Island. Each was dispatched from a company barge with 70 lb of lead tied to his feet. A few days later a severe storm struck the islands and damaged a number of houses. Local legend holds that these were the very houses of those people who had informed on Aspin and his friend, and the storm became known as *Ribut Aspin* (Aspin's storm).

During its peak population period in the 1930s and 1940s, the settlement extended much further to the north, east and all along the windy southern shore. A grassy area north of the present settlement was fenced off and used for grazing a large flock of sheep. Long seawalls were built that enclosed sheltered ponds on the lagoon side of the island. These held fish and turtles and protected the settlement from the ravages of storm surges, several of which are reported to have passed right across the island. The remnants of these breakwaters provide a safe anchorage for the island's many small vessels.

During World War II a detachment of Royal Marines set up camp on Home Island, close to the copra sheds. To pass their time these servicemen organised and played a great deal of sport. They played soccer against the islanders and against military teams from other islands. They travelled to Horsburgh to play cricket and hockey against the Ceylonese troops stationed there. Concrete tennis courts and a nine-hole golf course with four sand greens were constructed on Home Island. The course followed an L-shape from the present day central square back to the eastern shore and then turned south to *Ujung Waru* (Hibiscus Point, the southern arm of the island). Island youngsters were paid in cigarettes if they found any missing balls in the scrub!

News of the Japanese capture of Singapore in 1942 reached the islands via the cable and wireless station on Direction Island. A few ex-Cocos Islanders were killed during the seizure and it seemed as if a rapid Japanese advance to the south was inevitable. Trenches were dug at the southern end of the island and a warning siren was sounded each morning. People would leave their places of work and take shelter behind sandbags as Japanese reconnaissance aircraft from Singapore swept over the islands on a regular basis. When Direction Island was bombarded by a Japanese vessel in 1942 the Home Island community took flight to South Island. Here many built *atap* (frond) huts and sailed to work each day.

In August 1944 Home Island was bombed and strafed by a Japanese aircraft. The contingent of Royal Marines was caught out on the golf course at the time — far away from their small but effective anti-aircraft guns. Two bombs fell in the lagoon but another flattened houses in the vicinity of the present school. It killed a Cocos woman named Minti binte Sedaya and a boy, Edet bin Amro. The plane then dumped fuel onto the community and swept low over the palms with machine guns blazing. Twenty-seven houses were destroyed and people again fled to South Island.

Oceania House, the old Clunies-Ross family mansion, still stands on the south-western corner of the island, its glistening, white glazed brick frontage belying its age. A foundation stone declares that it was designed and built by George Clunies Ross in 1893. Imported timbers and numerous paintings grace much of the interior. The grand scale of its construction and the surrounding gardens clearly reflect the prosperity and status of its former inhabitants. A huge, but crumbling old wall with broken glass set into the top surrounds the compound and speaks silently of the earlier division between the family on the inside and their workers on the outside. Today, paying guests may savour the comforts of a bygone era, as the *rumah besar* (big house) is currently being developed as a tourist facility.

This corner of the island was once graced by a large fruit tree that local legend recalls as a 'talking tree'. Unfortunately it was blown down by a cyclone around the turn of the century. Such trees feature quite frequently in the legends of Asia and the Arab world.

A central village square was created on Home Island in the 1950s into which the three community mosques were placed. These were earlier located at the back of the *kampong*, beside the playing field. A fourth mosque, belonging to the former contracted labourers and situated at the northern extremity of the community, was not rebuilt after its *imam* moved to North Borneo.

Water is pumped up from an underground 'lens' of fresh water and power supply has recently been augmented by the installation of a huge wind-generator, aligned to pick up the almost constant south-easterly trade winds.

For most of its history the community's fortunes have depended on the vagaries of the copra industry. The commercial viability of this abundant island product finally came to an

Home Island, 1945, showing damage (centre right) from Japanese air-raid in 1944 (*Courtesy A. de Groot, U.K.*)

end in 1987. The industry used to employ a large number of women. Each day they could be seen chopping through the hard inner coconut shells, levering out the fleshy contents and laying it out to dry on racks in the sun. The process was further extended by the use of hot drying ovens. The dried copra was then bagged, stored and loaded onto visiting ships bound for Singapore.

Today the former copra workers are far more gainfully employed developing fruit, vegetable and poultry resources for the territory. An area near the former copra sheds has been converted into a large horticultural plot growing labour-intensive crops such as tomatoes, chillies, capsicums and beans. Alongside this area are large chicken and pigeon-raising enclosures. Pigeon meat has a taste very similar to that of migratory sea-birds, and is being developed as a dietary alternative to the protected species.

A small museum, focusing on the environment, crafts and culture of the Cocos Malay people, was officially opened on Home Island in 1987. Here, several fine examples of locally designed sailing craft never fail to draw comment from visitors. The steadily increasing number of displays covers local vegetation, shells, household utensils, old photographs, antique *wayang kulit* (shadow puppets), wedding costumes and even the old plastic money-making machine. This device and its products became the centre of international attention in the 1970s, for these worthless pieces of plastic could only be spent in the Clunies-Ross store. They could not be converted into legal tender and were useless beyond the shores of Home Island.

Today the affairs of the community are in the hands of a freely elected seven-member council and the Australian federal government. The community's business interests are looked after by a cooperative society, to which most of the working population belong.

Windswept southern shore of South Island, with hikers on a low-tide trek around the islands.

SOUTH ISLAND

South Island originally comprised a number of smaller islands. These have gradually coalesced over time. The former breaks are still evident in the two narrow, boulder-strewn, infertile sections of the island near its south-eastern elbow. No freshwater 'lens' exists beneath these sections, whereas the bulbous parts of the island are well supplied with underground water.

The seaward sides of this very long island receive the full blast of the prevailing winds. Its beaches are wild and windswept, while its inner shores are sheltered and muddy. The island is locally referred to as *Pulu Atas* or 'top island'. The Cocos Malay people generally refer to places being 'up or down wind', something far more locally relevant than the cardinal points of the compass.

The middle section of this island, *Kabun Jerok* (orange grove), was chosen by Captain John Clunies Ross in 1827 as the site for his first settlement. Had Alexander Hare not departed the scene and left him with the far better situated Home Island, one wonders whether Captain Clunies Ross would have been able to survive on this rather inaccessible southern isle. He had almost no choice in the matter of his first site, however, as all the other major islands were under Hare's control at the time of his arrival. He dredged out a number of boating channels through the coral to reach South Island, but even then access must have been very hard at low tides.

Early maps of the islands soon after settlement show two fishermen's huts on stilts over the shallow sandy flats in the lee of South Island. One is labelled as belonging to Alexander Hare, the other to Clunies Ross. They were so close together that one can only think that the newer one must have been sited there solely out of rivalry.

South Island has long been favoured as a popular weekend camping place. The early Clunies Rosses and their managers maintained small huts on this island and would visit whenever they could. The old boat channels were maintained for easy access by the periodic hand-raking of the coral by teams of workers. *Atap* huts were also constructed here for the sufferers of the disease known as beri-beri. It was believed that the daily exercise of walking on stones would help them regain strength in their legs. Turn-of-the-century medicine was not aware that this ailment stemmed from a vitamin deficiency.

A small settlement was established on the island in World War II when a regiment of Kenyan soldiers, the Fifth African Rifles, set up camp by the sheltered bay on the island's south-western shore. Their job was to keep a

look-out for ships at sea and raise the Union Jack if one was sighted. A small building for this purpose was erected on the top of the prominent sandhill known locally as the *Gunung* (mountain). There were four other such Admiralty Flag Watcher stations around the island chain and the task was later taken over by the Islanders.

South Island has some of the highest land of the territory. Large wind-blown dunes rise steeply from the southern and eastern shores. The *Gunung* near the south-western corner of the island reaches a height of nine metres. It provides protection for a peaceful bay often fancied by weekend campers from West Island. This imposing sand-dune figures largely in local legend, as does any really prominent or unusual natural feature. A depression on the inland side of the dune is believed to be inhabited by an evil *setan* (spirit) and very few Cocos Malay people will visit this spot willingly. The *setan* is said to have gathered together the lost spirits of any individuals who have disappeared without trace in local waters. Sabarin bin Rapayi, an experienced boatman who had helped to sail

Nek Renja with his *jukong* and hut at *Kabun Jerok* on the sheltered lagoon side of South Island

the *Rainbow* out from England earlier this century, failed to return one day after visiting South Island. He had gone there alone and without his *parang*. His *jukong* was later found, but there was no trace of him.

South Island is today dotted with a dozen or so *pondok*, or weekender shacks, belonging to extended family groupings in the Malay community. A flock of chickens is kept and regularly fed at each hut. When the tides suit, whole families camp in these huts and spend most of their waking hours hunting and gathering the island's natural resources. Fish, spider-shells, clams, *kepala biola* (a shell-fish), coconuts and firewood are amassed and transported home, to then be shared out among family and friends. Malay women often spend long hours beneath the trees stripping coconut fronds to make their *penyapu* (swish brooms). Mud crabs of huge proportions can be taken from the mud-flats at low tide and crayfish are abundant on the outer reef at night.

Every point, bay and natural feature on the island has its own Malay name. Near *Kabun Jerok* is an old, seldom-visited well hidden deep in the island's undergrowth. Malay elders recount that no leaf has ever fallen into this well and that its cool, clear, pure water has youth-giving properties. The schooner named the *Harriet* was built near *Kebun Geronggang* in 1835, utilising the formerly abundant supply of Ironwood. A small copra-producing settlement was maintained near *Rumah Nek Net*, under the supervision of a Scottish overseer and his Malay wife.

The southern shore of the island has been the downfall of at least two vessels in recent times. In the early hours of 10 May 1969 the 16-ton Danish schooner, *Sawan-kha-loke* was washed across the reef. Fortunately, she did not sustain a great deal of damage. She was eventually winched up over the dunes and refloated in the lagoon. An American ketch, the *Seaweed*, was not so fortunate. She ran onto the same wild coastal strip during the early hours of 25 August 1977 and was severely damaged on one side. The vessel stuck fast on the edge of the dunes and

remained a local landmark until late 1983 when a severe storm removed all but the lead from her keel.

Originally this island was thickly vegetated and had some fine stands of Ironwood and Pisonia. The remnants of these were cut for building materials earlier this century. Parts of the island are still littered with their huge stumps. A bulldozer track once ran the length of the island but this has long since become overgrown. The same bulldozer's track across the southern reef-flat from West Island is still very evident, however, and indicates the shallowest route for modern day inter-island hikers to follow.

WEST ISLAND

Known to the Cocos Malay people as *Pulu Panjang* (long island), West Island is the largest island in the territory. It was first settled by a contingent of Alexander Hare's people in 1826, but has not always been occupied. This first settlement is believed to have been in the vicinity of *Rumah Baru* (new house), in the north-east. Here the early settlers tended and cultivated tropical fruit and vegetable crops under the supervision of Charles Downie.

West Island almost splits into three distinct sections and may well have been three separate islands in the time before settlement. The northern section is closest to the deeper reaches of the lagoon and is now served by a wooden jetty. The Shell Oil Company of Australia has established a large fuel storage area at this end of the island, and a long underwater pipeline extends out into the lagoon to enable tankers to anchor and pump fuel supplies ashore.

Vertical view of West Island settlement (*Crown Copyright Australian Surveying and Land Information Group, Canberra*)

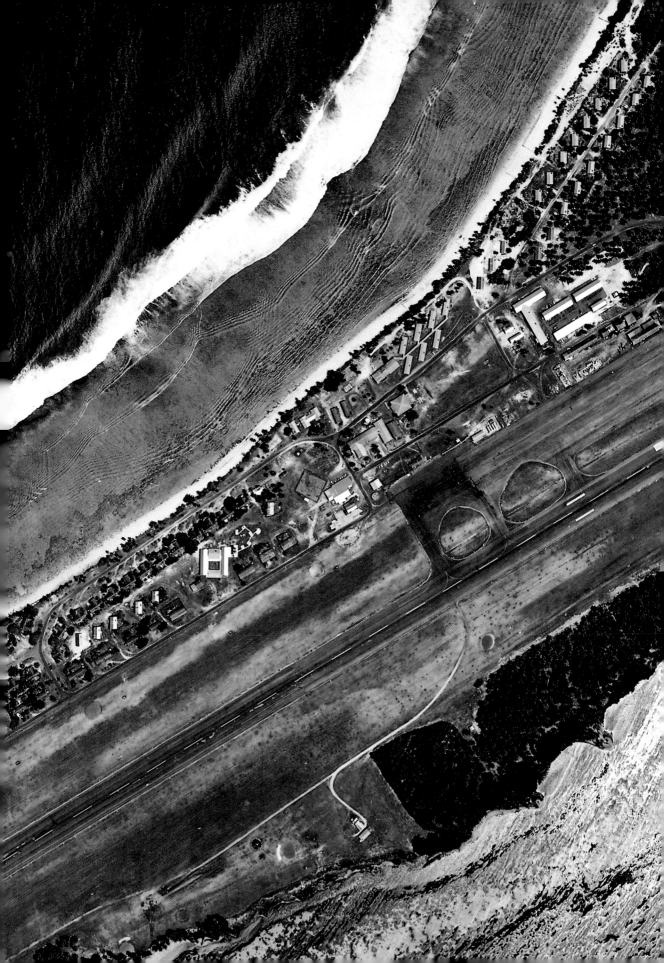

The *Rumah Baru* area features prominently in local history. In 1908, a Javanese contracted labourer by the name of Biong ran amok and was eventually captured near here. He was fed up with his living and working conditions and felt that he had been given false information at the time of his recruitment in Java. The final straw came when he was working in the garden of *Oceania House*. He looked up into a *jambu* tree and saw Bertha, one of John Sydney Clunies-Ross' mistresses. Harsh words were exchanged and the cheeky woman spat on him. He and his friend, Emon, then ran away to West Island in a stolen boat. Emon was captured near Trannies Beach, but Biong acted like a man possessed. He was speared and shot twice by the search party, but it still took a number of men to restrain him and get him into a *jukong*. Another Javanese settler, Nek Icang, is said to have finally subdued Biong by removing a 'magic sash' he was wearing around his waist. He died upon reaching Home Island. His friend Emon was locked up, whipped regularly and made to bathe in salt water. He died three weeks later.

The *Rumah Baru* area has served as a *jukong* landing site for a long time and is now the preferred power-boat launching site for West Islanders. Near here, in the 1950s, Ranet bin Geba and his sailing craft disappeared during a storm. Searchers only found his broken rudder. Evidence of wartime camps can be seen in this area. An old amphibious landing craft is rusting away in the thick bush, as is a conical-roofed circular tank believed to have been used for seawater desalination. A wartime well even has a population of tiny freshwater fish, whose ancestors must have been brought in by servicemen.

The lagoon floor near here abounds in large coral heads, the current is swift and the area is quite hazardous at low tide. Giant clams are said to have once been prevalent in this section of the lagoon, but have long since been collected for their tasty flesh.

Central West Island served as a coconut plantation until 1944 when it began to be transformed into an airstrip by the arrival of some 7000 British, Canadian, Australian and Indian military personnel. The place became a sudden hive of activity as trees were felled

Indian Army Engineers clear the plantation for 'Sydney Highway', a road linking the West Island jetty and the airstrip, 1945. (*Courtesy Imperial War Museum, London*)

and Marsden steel matting strips were steadily locked into place to form a runway. The community, known by the code-name SP129, boasted its own newspaper, *The Atoll*. The servicemen were paid a special visit by British wartime singer and comedienne, Gracie Fields, in 1945. Cocos was to have become a base from which an air assault on Japanese-held territories to the north was to have taken place. Spitfire aircraft arrived in crates and were assembled on the island. Mosquito aircraft made numerous photographic sorties from here to Singapore, Malaya and Java. These were followed by Liberator bombing missions.

Two Mosquitoes, a Liberator, a Spitfire and a Catalina flying-boat crashed on or close to Cocos during 1945. The two crewmen in each Mosquito managed to survive their crash-landings: one on North Keeling and one in *Telok Jambu* (North Lagoon) on West Island. The Spitfire crew were picked up by the air-sea rescue team, but Liberator EW 622 was lost without a trace to the south-west of West Island after take-off. Of the fourteen men on board Catalina JX 334, only five survived.

The sudden surrender of the Japanese in 1945 came as a surprise to all on Cocos. The newly completed airstrip had to be abandoned and tons of unwanted equipment was ditched over the outer Cocos reef. The military personnel were collected by a large number of troop-carrying ships and West Island slipped back into obscurity for a further six years. Some vehicles, hastily abandoned in the bushes by departing airmen, were later restored in the 1950s by enterprising West Islanders, who took great delight in driving them around the settlement.

Renewed interest in the airstrip came in 1951 when it was reclaimed from the encroaching vegetation and given a firm, crushed coral and concrete base. The old metal strips were gouged out and dumped in Telok Jambu, where they are still visible today. The new strip had to be capable of safely handling the big Qantas Constellations and Stratocruisers that were going to carry passengers across the Indian Ocean to and from South Africa. Along with the new airstrip came a small supporting community with Civil Aviation, Qantas, Shell, air-sea rescue and meteorological employees.

West Island runway under construction, 1945 (*Courtesy Imperial War Museum, London*)

Steadily the West Island mainlander community has grown in size and sophistication of services. Today it even sports a modern, four-bed hospital, complete with operating theatre. An air-conditioned supermarket is run by the Cocos Islands Cooperative and it provides an excellent range of household items for such a remote community.

In 1981 a 21.5 ha high-security Animal Quarantine Station was opened on the western 'elbow' of West Island. High quality overseas sheep, goats, and cattle are staged through Cocos on their way to mainland Australian buyers. The animals arrive by ship, specially converted aircraft or as frozen embryos ready for transfer into Australian host animals. All will then spend a number of months on Cocos under very strict scrutiny. Forage sorghum is grown on site and the station is equipped with a highly sophisticated laboratory and associated facilities.

The central part of West Island contains the airstrip and the expatriate Australian community. Some 250 mainlanders live here for the duration of two to three year contracts. The community is well serviced and is well equipped with social and sporting facilities. The fringes of the airstrip serve as an eighteen-hole golf course and there are regular tournaments. An active tennis club meets under floodlights once a week. Other clubs include rifle-shooting, scuba diving, surfing, sailing, darts and fishing. Social life on West Island revolves around the Cocos Club, a large cyclone shelter that doubles as a recreation centre. Regular videos, dinners, amateur dramatics and special 'club-nights' are held with the added incentive of duty-free alcohol.

Residents of West Island are mainly government workers who are employed in maintenance and construction work, aviation communications, island administration, quarantine services, meteorological observation, health services, retailing and education.

Above:
Meteorological observer
prepares a weather
balloon for launching

Right:
Animal Quarantine
Station, West Island

The island provides a wonderful environment for children and resourceful adults. Many West Island families own small power boats and enjoy weekend picnic and camping excursions to other islands. A complete primary and secondary schooling is provided and a locally based radio station is manned by volunteer disc jockeys. A hectic annual calendar of social activities includes such events as a three-week festival of sport known as the 'Cocos Olympics', a mid-year ball and hermit crab race meetings.

The islands are served by a weekly chartered aircraft from Perth, and its arrival each week is a big social occasion. During its one hour on the ground, eagerly awaited mail, newspapers, magazines, fresh fruit and vegetables are unloaded. Family visitors and friends are then given an emotional send-off.

The island's southern arm is clothed in relatively recently planted coconut palms and boasts two popular shelling and picnic spots. If the tide is particularly high, access to the southern extremity can be difficult. Picnickers and visitors to the Yacht Club at South End are sometimes stranded there until the water subsides.

A short distance across a shallow passage is the tiny island of *Pulu Maria*. This popular fishing spot is named after one of two European children who disappeared without trace from its shores in the 1860s. Local legend believes their ghosts to have been taken to South Island by the evil *setan* that lives there behind the *Gunung*.

Left:
A VISTA and INMARSAT satellite communications system provides 24-hour telephone and facsimile connection to the rest of the world

Bottom left:
'Charter Day' is the busiest day of the week on Cocos

Bottom right:
Cocos scouts pay their respects at the annual Anzac Day ceremony

Another small island close to South End is *Pulu Kambing*, named after the goats that were once kept there. It served as a cremation and burial place for Indian and British servicemen who died on Cocos during World War II. Injured servicemen arrived here by aircraft and were treated at a wartime hospital near present-day Scout Park.

A memorial at John's Rock marks the site where Edward Twiss was lost, presumed drowned, in 1970. An Aviation employee, he was apparently looking for crayfish along this dangerous section of reef. A severed leg was all that was later recovered. The memorial also marks the probable site of the wreck of the brig, *Sir Francis Nicholas Burton*, which ran aground on the southern shore in 1826.

This island has seen its share of tragedy over the years. A small graveyard just south of the Quarantine Station marks the final resting place of a cable station employee, a community doctor, a West Island resident and a German seaman who succumbed to the injuries he sustained in an engine room explosion. A group of memorials behind the single-

Part of West Island settlement, 1983, showing single quarters (foreground), club and administration block (centre), the airstrip and visiting RAAF aircraft (*Courtesy Royal Australian Air Force*)

persons' mess recalls three separate incidents of accidental drowning during which ten servicemen were lost in 1945.

HORSBURGH ISLAND

Pulu Luar, the 'outside island', is not easily accessible by boat because of a sweep of reef that almost encircles it. High tides provide an opportunity for entry from the south-east, although the passage is littered with large coral heads. Difficulty of access does not, however, seem to have hampered its almost continual occupation by a variety of settlers from 1826 until the close of World War II.

Alexander Hare posted a group of people here to grow fruit and vegetables. Their numbers steadily increased as Hare progressively transferred his workers to here from other islands. Their frequent contact with the Clunies Ross party on South Island was not to his liking, and Horsburgh is the only island in the southern group that is inaccessible by foot at low tide.

Some time after Hare's departure from the atoll, Horsburgh Island again became a place of exile. This time it was for single women and unmarried mothers. Their task was the same as that of its first occupants — to grow vegetables for the Home Island community. After the opening of the cable station on Direction Island in 1901, their vegetable 'market' expanded to include this smaller settlement. Single women were usually posted to Horsburgh for a year, but some were kept there for much longer.

Some of the Horsburgh women were put to work making coconut oil, soap, coir mats and ropes. Leave was granted to the sick and to those invited to family ceremonies on Home Island. The whole group would return for the *Hari Raya* festival and New Year celebrations. The womens' salaries were kept for them on Home Island and they were able to make financial contributions to their families whenever they wished.

Horsburgh Island, looking south-east

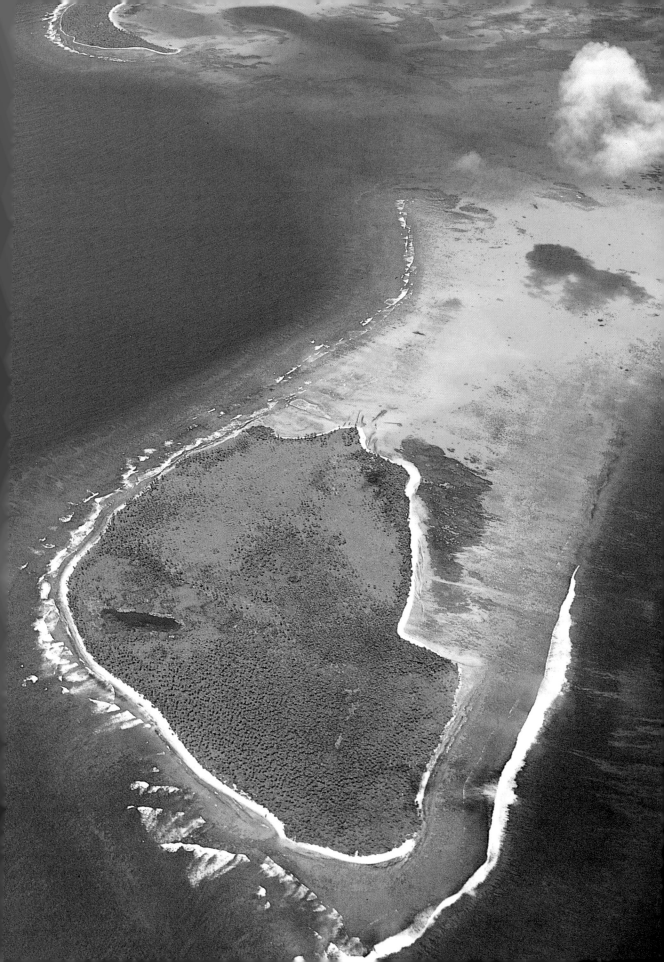

Visitors to Horsburgh were discouraged, but the small boats that called regularly to collect their produce also brought them food, gifts and proposals of marriage from people in the *kampong* on Home Island. The women and their married-couple supervisors lived in a long-house and are said to have lived quite well, apart from their isolation and the occasional mysterious pregnancy!

For a while George Clunies Ross kept and bred herds of imported Rusa and Kidang Deer on Horsburgh Island. These were hunted down and shot for sport. George maintained a holiday house on the island's windy eastern-most point. His son, John Sydney, also enjoyed this family retreat and would stay there most weekends and some nights during the week. He loved the island's wildlife, especially the delicate White Terns and the tiny Silver Eyes that were introduced from Christmas Island. He prohibited members of the *kampong* from taking any fish, crayfish, turtles and birds from this island. Its wildlife could only be taken by its permanent residents for their immediate needs.

An unusual feature on the island is the clump of mangroves that occupies the northern shore of its shallow, brackish lake. In the warm, salty waters of the small lake they have found the ideal conditions in which to develop. They are not found anywhere else in the Territory.

This island's relative tranquility was interrupted by the advent of World War II. In November 1940 a secret report by a visiting Australian Army detachment expressed the view that Cocos should guard against another *Emden*-type incident. They recommended that a military presence be speedily arranged for the atoll. In 1941 Captain Koch of the Ceylon Garrison Artillery came to Cocos and his unit installed two six-inch guns on Hors-burgh Island to protect the atoll's main entrance and anchorage. This installation was to be supplemented by an infantry presence on Direction Island to protect the cable station. The men who would provide the islands' defences were to come from two volunteer corps, the Ceylon Light Infantry and the Ceylon Garrison Artillery.

The young men who came to Cocos later that year were the first contingents of Ceylonese volunteers ever to do overseas service. They were fresh out of private schools, hungry for action and not at all ready for British military discipline. Some came to Cocos after a short posting to the Seychelles, where they had caused some disquiet by suggesting that German prisoners of war were better treated than 'coloured' soldiers.

These troops found their six months on 'Island X', as Cocos was known, to be an eternity made doubly worse by the appointment of British officers above Singhalese and Burgher (Anglo-Ceylonese) men. To ease their boredom they played cricket and listened to the English-language broadcasts on Japanese radio. This fuelled their anti-colonial feelings even more. From these broadcasts they learned of a frightening sequence of events to their north:

15 February (1942) — Singapore surrendered to Japan

19 February — Japanese bombed Darwin

8 March — Jakarta surrendered to Japan

31 March — the Japanese took Christmas Island after a mutiny by Indian troops

5 April — Japanese air raid on Colombo

9 April — Japanese air raid on ships in Trincomalee harbour, Ceylon

These events, together with a shelling of Direction Island on 3 March, convinced the young volunteers that the Japanese were on their way to Cocos. Led by Gratien Fernando, a group of CGA gunners decided to overthrow

World War II Ceylonese gun emplacement on Horsburgh Island

their despised British officers, make contact with the Japanese and hand over the islands to them in a bloodless mutiny.

The events of the night of 8 May 1942 are not well recorded. It seems that things did not go as planned. Soldiers who were expected to be asleep were still awake, the duty observer strongly resisted the mutineers and was killed, the bren gun that was commandeered jammed in the middle of the take-over bid and would-be supporters ran away into the bushes. Several men were injured, including the second-in-command, Lt. Henry Stephens. A court martial was hastily convened the next morning by Capt. George Gardiner. Messages were sent to the officers commanding the CLI on Direction Island to come across immediately as there had been 'a little trouble'. Seven mutineers were sentenced to death by firing squad and the verdict was cabled to Colombo.

The higher authorities were not happy with the composition and the conduct of the court martial and asked that all the accused men be held on Direction Island until they could be sent back for retrial. An Indian warship, the *Jumna*, later collected them. Their subsequent trial was held in the Supreme Court in Colombo and was for murder, not mutiny. Four gunners were imprisoned and three were hanged. The youngest mutineer, Carlo Gauder, was executed on his twenty-first birthday.

In October 1944 the British Colonial Office secretly arranged to have the ageing Sultan of Selangor brought to Cocos for fear that he might become a puppet ruler for the Japanese and the focus of further unrest in Malaya. Raja Musa Eddin and his wife, Tengku Mastora, brought a number of retainers with them and lived in exile on Horsburgh Island under the protection of the British until the end of the war.

The estate provided the Sultan with a fisherman named Apna. Cocos Malay boatmen would deliver messages and provisions once or twice a week. Apart from

Lagoon waters swirl
around tiny Prison
Island

these brief contacts, there was little interaction with the Home Islanders. Nevertheless, they believed the Sultan and his wife to possess psychic powers. English officers who at first despised him were seen to 'come under his spell' and make more and more frequent visits to his camp. His sponsorship of Apna's winning *jukong* in the *Hari Raya* boat races was additional proof of his strength. This lengthy stay by Malay royalty on Horsburgh Island left a lasting impression on the inhabitants.

Two rusted gun emplacements remain on the southern point today as reminders of the military occupation of Horsburgh Island. The barrel of one is intact, while the other has rolled onto the beach and is covered with sand. The grave of Gunner Samuel Jayasekera can still be seen in the centre of the island, although his body was exhumed in 1958. An

overgrown cricket pitch is visible only from the air and some military wells are still useable. Apart from these small reminders, almost nothing remains of the human dramas that have taken place on this island.

Horsburgh today is unoccupied and is used mainly as a limited seabird-shooting venue. The flesh of these seabirds is a rather salty delicacy in the diet of the island people. West Islanders occasionally camp on Horsburgh and enjoy diving on its colourful, but shark-infested reefs.

A shipwreck is visible at low tide on the sandbank to the south-east of Horsburgh island. This is the *Pheaton*, a three-masted English barque that was run aground in 1889 after a fire in her hold could not be contained. Today it is occupied by myriads of coloured fish and is another favourite spot with local divers.

DIRECTION ISLAND

Regarded by many as the most scenic island in the Cocos Keeling group, Direction Island or 'D.I.', bears little witness today to its important place in local and international history. An old jetty, some concrete slabs and the remains of a supply store are all that is left to remind us of the vital role it played in world communications earlier this century.

This island can claim to have hosted the first ever human occupation of the atoll, for it was here that Le Cour and his fellow shipwrecked sailors from the *Mauritius* camped for a number of months in 1825. It was later occupied by a party of Alexander Hare's people, but the settlement was fairly short-lived. Later attempts were made to try to cultivate vegetables here using soil imported from Christmas Island, but these gardens were hampered by a lack of underground water. The island is too narrow to possess a fresh water 'lens'.

Von Mucke and the German raiders leave Direction Island jetty to take charge of the schooner, *Ayesha*, 1914.
(*Courtesy Imperial War Museum, London*)

Around the turn of the century, Lloyds of London negotiated with the Clunies Ross estate to set up a tall mast on the north-western tip of Direction Island for the purpose of signalling to passing ships. A two-roomed brick hut was to be erected for the watchman and the storage of signal flags. However, the flagstaff was never used and it is not certain that the building was ever completed. This part of the island has since become known as Ruin Point.

At the same time as the signalling negotiations with Lloyds, Direction Island was in the process of being connected to Cottesloe in Western Australia by an undersea telegraphic cable. The Eastern Extension Telegraph Company then opened a cable repeater station on the island in 1901. The installation had a staff of 29 Englishmen and a number of Chinese, Indian and Singaporean Malay workmen. In 1911 the telegraph service was augmented by a wireless facility and in 1914 the island was Australia's only communication link with the rest of the British Empire.

The vital undersea cable linkages to Singapore and South Africa made Cocos a natural

focus of enemy interest. In November 1914 the powerful wireless plant was keeping in touch with all allied shipping in the Indian Ocean, including a convoy of 38 ANZAC troopships bound for the Middle East under the protection of *HMAS Melbourne*, *HMAS Sydney* and the Japanese cruiser, *Ibuki*.

Early on the morning of 9 November a German cruiser, *SMS Emden*, was spotted by an alert Chinese servant. The elusive raider was steaming towards Cocos, intent on destroying the cable and wireless communications. The servant told the telegraph operator on duty about the approaching ship and he immediately cabled Singapore. The wireless operator then called the Australian fleet. The message was brief, 'S.O.S. *Emden* here'. The station then fell silent.

A landing party of 50 men led by First Officer Hellmuth von Mücke came ashore with orders to destroy the cable station. His party wrecked every instrument they could find. They blew up the engine room, lopped the wireless mast and chopped a dummy cable into short, souvenir lengths. Suddenly three sharp blasts on the *Emden*'s siren called them away from their looting.

The raiders reboarded their landing craft but could not reach their mother ship before Captain Karl von Müller had to swing her around to meet the *HMAS Sydney*. Von Müller had at first thought the *Sydney* was his own collier, the *Buresk*, and had reacted a little slowly to the appearance of the Australian warship.

As the cable and wireless men watched from their remaining rooftops, the two ships locked horns in a fight to the death. The Germans scored the first hits, but once the Australian vessel had moved out of her enemy's firing range she was able to land many successful salvoes on the *Emden*'s decks and superstructure. Von Müller was forced to drive his ship onto the fringing reefs of North Keeling Island in order to avoid sinking. There he stuck fast while the *Sydney* turned to engage the German collier. The crew of the *Buresk* had already scuttled their vessel and the *Sydney* lowered two lifeboats

for the swimming crewmen. Back on North Keeling, von Müller was reluctant to surrender until a few more well-placed hits convinced him to run up a white flag.

On Direction Island the raiders had realised the worst. They grabbed many boxes of supplies and announced that they would commandeer the Clunies Ross schooner, *Ayesha*, lying at anchor in the bay. This they did before the *Sydney* returned and their subsequent escape all the way back to Germany became one of the most incredible adventure stories of the entire war.

The cable station staff were congratulated on their speed of reaction to the attack, their foresight in burying spare equipment and in laying a false cable. Their installation was back in working order within a day of the raid.

After a period of reconstruction, life on the cable station settled down again. Water supply remained a constant problem and huge rainwater tanks were installed in addition to seawater condenser units. A new radio mast went up in 1918 and a second, more modern cable was laid in 1926. The station men were the typical colonial Englishmen of the time, who played tennis and billiards, dressed for dinner and were attended by a large number of retainers. They had gardeners, painters, laundrymen, boatmen, waiters, houseboys and clerical assistants. Staff were divided into junior and senior ranks and their non-English retainers lived in huts at the back of the island.

The Clunies Ross family and their managers had frequent interaction with the cable station. The Cocos Malay people also had a degree of contact and were permitted to barter food with station employees in the years prior to World War II. Indeed, a number of Chinese and Indian station employees married local Malay women. The only proviso made was that the couple would have to leave the islands. The staff of the cable station also included a doctor, who would attend to urgent cases on Home Island. The Clunies Ross estate recruited cablemen as managers and Rose Clunies-Ross, widow of John Sydney, later married a cable station employee. Social relations between the estate and the cable station varied enormously over the years, however, depending very much on the particular personalities involved.

Hosman bin Awang, a Singaporean Malay, came to Cocos as a cable station employee soon after World War I. He married a Cocos girl and took her back to Singapore. The marriage proved unsuccessful, however, and he returned to the cable station for another tour of duty a few years later. He then married a second Cocos Malay girl and was granted permission to live on Home Island. Here he conducted a small school for island boys for fifteen years before leaving for Christmas Island in 1951.

The cable station became a wartime target again on 3 March 1942. A Japanese vessel had approached the island from behind and shelled the installation from quite short range. Fires raged everywhere, but unbeknown to the enemy, most of these were bonfires built up in readiness to destroy documents in the event of an invasion. Their light lit up the whole atoll. The buildings suffered some damage, but it must have appeared as though the entire facility had been knocked out, for the enemy vessel sailed away without sending anyone ashore. A Chinese carpenter was killed in the incident, but there was no actual damage to the cables. With the consent of British Admiralty, the cable station arranged for a false wireless message in plain language to be sent to Batavia (Jakarta), advising staff there to disconnect their cable instruments as Direction Island had been 'permanently put out of action'. The message was intercepted by the Japanese and was accepted. The word 'Cocos' was not used again for the rest of the war and false shell holes were painted on the cable station's rooftops to maintain the deception.

During peacetime, passing passenger liners would often come in close to the islands, wave to the cablemen on shore and drop a barrel of fresh foodstuffs and mail over the side for collection by Malay *jukongs*. This tradition became known as the 'Cocos Barrel' and began in 1909 with the passage of the P & O liner *Morea* and continued until 1954 with such well-known ships as the *Orontes*, the *Orion* and the *Strathaird*. Sometimes an exchange of barrels was extremely difficult in rough seas. Once, the *Strathaird* had to haul the Cocos people aboard and take them on to Fremantle.

Until 1944 there was no airstrip on Cocos. When Japan entered World War II, aircraft contact between Australia and Asia became very difficult. There were very few planes in existence that could make the long 'hops' between Australia and East Africa or Ceylon. A proving flight in 1939 by Captain P.G. Taylor showed that Catalina flying boats were quite capable of crossing the vast expanse of the Indian Ocean, as long as refuelling stops were provided. In March 1942 a Dutch Air Force Catalina, attempting such a crossing, was forced to land on the Cocos lagoon. There she struck a coral head and tore a large hole in her undercarriage. With assistance from a large number of Home Islanders the craft was towed ashore on Direction Island, a huge patch was made and she took off again within hours, to the utter amazement of the estate workers.

A Royal Air Force squadron of these long-range amphibious aircraft was formed in Koggala, Ceylon, in July 1942. They subsequently succeeded in making 824 secret crossings of the Indian Ocean to Perth. Their missions included anti-shipping patrols, air-sea rescue sorties, submarine strikes, personnel movements and official mail runs. Their non-stop flight time was 28 hours. When carrying larger payloads these aircraft refuelled at Cocos.

Recovering from the ravages
of the Indian Ocean,
Direction Island anchorage

Their 'landing strip' was the section of water immediately in front of Direction and Prison Islands. Qantas Empire Airways maintained a fleet of five Catalinas that were also frequent visitors to Cocos. One of these was resting on the lagoon on 14 February 1944 when it was spotted by a Japanese reconnaissance aircraft. It dropped a single bomb from a great height which narrowly missed the moored aircraft. For some reason no further bombing attacks were made on the outpost for another six months.

With the increase in military aircraft activity at Cocos, it was necessary to establish an air-sea rescue base. Direction Island was selected as the best site because of its natural anchorage. The high-speed launch rescue service was operated by the RAF and its main purpose was the quick recovery of men and equipment from any aircraft that had ditched in the vicinity of the islands. Any ailing flying boats were speedily serviced and refuelled from here as well. The base was equipped with three high-speed launches. A concrete slipway was constructed towards the southern end of the island, utilising nineteenth century ex-Indian Railway tracks from the cable station. Iron rails now stretched from one end of the island to the other. Water still posed a problem, so the island's supplies were supplemented with desalinated water piped from a condenser near *Rumah Baru* on West Island into water-carrying boats.

Fortunately, there were very few rescue calls during the eighteen-month life of the base. The most tragic episode occurred on 27 June 1945 when Catalina JX 334 hit a wave on landing and caught fire. The aircraft sank so quickly that seven men were trapped inside. Of the remaining seven, two later died in the small hospital on Direction Island.

Just as the airstrip on West Island was resurrected in the 1950s, so too was the air-sea rescue facility on Direction Island. Manned by eight young Australians from the Department of Aviation, the base was equipped with six large vessels and it remained in operation until 1969. Regular day and night patrols were maintained over a range of 500 miles. Most of the calls for assistance came from passing ships with sick or injured passengers and crew. There were very few aircraft rescues.

With the Australian takeover of Cocos in 1955, the staffing of the cable station gradually changed from English to Australian personnel. Five prefabricated houses were made in Australia and shipped to the islands for reassembly on Direction Island. These houses were dismantled when the cable station closed in 1966 and were moved to West Island, where they can still be seen with their wide verandahs looking out over the airstrip. The air-sea rescue unit's huge boatshed was also relocated after the base closed and can now be seen at the head of the main boat-slip on Home Island. All other buildings, pathways, railway lines and unwanted equipment on Direction Island were bulldozed into the sea at the back of the island in the late 1960s. The island was then completely replanted with coconut palms.

Direction Island today is a favorite anchorage for around-the-world yachts. In the months between March and November anything up to 20 ocean-going sailing craft will be seen at anchor here in the bay. The sheltered blue waters of the lagoon provide them with a welcome haven from the vast Indian Ocean. One unfortunate yacht still lies on the bottom of this bay, however, and is easily reached by snorkellers. This is the *Lady Esther II*, a large American cruising yacht that was burnt to the water-line in an accidental fire on 21 October 1979. Only the non-swimming wife of the owner and her tiny dog were aboard at the time. They were found clinging to the anchor rope and were rescued.

At the southern extremity of the island is a channel of fast-moving water known locally as 'The Rip'. No spear or line fishing is permitted in this area, as it is a sanctuary for all marine life. For the strong-swimming snorkeller, a ride down 'The Rip' is an experience never to be forgotten. An enormous moray eel may make an occasional appearance on the rocky southern bank of the channel amid large greenfish, bass, schools of sweetlip and the odd black-tipped reef shark. This windy passage is a particular favourite with any West Islanders who go across to 'D.I.' for picnics.

In the not-too-distant future this island, known as *Pulu Tikus* (rat island) to the Cocos Malay people, may again become a focus of international attention. There are plans afoot to develop it into a high-class tourist resort, utilising wind power and a desalinated water-supply.

PRISON ISLAND

Prison Island, now a tiny button of land between Direction and Home Islands, was once twice its present size and possessed a hill that rivalled the large dune on South Island for the highest point of the atoll. Over the past 30 years, since the joining of *Pulu Gangsa* and Home Island, it has been eroded down to its present size.

The character of the island changes constantly as the tides and currents swirl the water around it. Its shores seem alternately covered in soft, white sand and sharp coral boulders.

This tiny island was indeed a 'prison' in the early years of settlement. The pioneer settler, Alexander Hare, moved his household here from Home Island some time after the arrival of John Clunies Ross in 1827. Hare's immediate 'family' was composed of a dozen young women and roughly 30 children. He had a number of buildings constructed for him on the island. One or two of these held the settlement's stores of rice and other provisions. Some smaller huts with a surrounding fence were built to house the children and Hare lived in a two-storeyed residence. He stayed in the upper level of this house in a sparsely furnished room and his young women lived down below. His earlier life in the East Indies had been one of adventure, influence and prestige. It would seem as though he was trying to see out the later days of his life in the style of an oriental rajah.

His workers were housed on other islands and were not allowed to visit *Pulu Tuan* (the master's island) without permission. Even his

supervisor, Mr Ogilvie, lived on Direction Island. Every ten days rationed provisions would be issued to the workers from the Prison Island stores. This would not include any allocation for children. Hare wanted to keep all the youngsters with him, possibly as surety for good behaviour. He would periodically issue one or two women as brides for men he wished to reward.

When Hare left the atoll in 1831, his house was abandoned. So sturdily was it built, that parts of it were still visible on the island until the turn of the century.

In Malay the island is known as *Pulu Beras* or 'rice island'. There are several explanations for this. One tells of a visiting supply ship last century that was bearing the settlement's stores of rice. It was holed and listing badly, so its precious cargo was hastily off-loaded onto this tiny island. Another explanation relates to the fact that Hare kept all of his rice there and a third story suggests that the island itself looks like a pile of spilled rice.

The Cocos Malay people say that the island is a very 'cold' place and that it is far too chilly for camping. The coldness is partly attributed to the presence of a mermaid. This legendary creature and her island are said to call back home any Cocos-born people who leave these shores. The original height of the island, topped by tall coconut palms, made it the last visible point of Cocos seen by anyone sailing to Java. A daughter of George Clunies Ross, Nonagati, is said to have never really settled in England because of her haunting memories of Prison Island.

NORTH KEELING ISLAND

Despite 150 years of nutting and timber collecting, the island of North Keeling remains substantially the same as it was in 1609 when it was spotted by Captain William Keeling. Its remoteness from the main atoll, its difficult landing area and the absence of a good, fresh-water supply have combined to preclude any possibility of permanent settlement. Nevertheless, small groups of Malay boats have paid occasional visits to this island practically every year since the early days of the occupation of the southern atoll. These hazardous voyages were usually made to collect coconuts, timber and seabirds.

Late in the nineteenth century, small camps of beri-beri sufferers were maintained on this island for short periods, the belief being that walking on the rocky shores would be beneficial to their condition. Twin Malay graves near the southern shore of the island mark the final resting places of a woman and a girl who succumbed to this dietary deficiency. Another beri-beri sufferer, Nek Katek, met an awful death when he was trapped in the soft sands of the central lagoon and covered by the rising tide. His body was recovered and buried in the south-eastern section of the island, known ever since as *Kuburan Nek Katek* (Nek Katek's grave).

In November 1914 the *SMS Emden* ran herself aground on the windswept southern reef after her unsuccessful encounter with *HMAS Sydney*. Many of the survivors attempted to swim to shore, but not all succeeded. Those who reached land were racked with thirst, and some died from drinking seawater. The *Sydney* returned the next day and took as many willing survivors aboard as she could.

Not all were prepared to give themselves up, unfortunately, and a handful of diehards hid in the forest and were left behind. Later that month it became the duty of the sloop, *HMAS Cadmus*, to bury the German dead on North Keeling. In January 1915 the *Cadmus* returned to the wreck and relieved it of 500 Mexican dollars, two guns and their mountings, one torpedo, a searchlight and numerous other items now on show in a naval museum in Sydney, Australia.

In October 1915 a work gang from Home Island found a number of skeletons which they buried on the shore near the wreck. One of these, still wearing his uniform with a pipe in his mouth, was found in the narrow south-western part of the island, sitting in the fork of a tree. The poor fellow must have died of thirst. This part of the island has become known as *Kuburan Bosun* (bosun's grave) ever since.

SMS Emden aground on North Keeling Island, 1914 (*Courtesy Imperial War Museum, London*)

From October 1915 to January 1916 the islanders salvaged what they could from the German ship. A cable was strung from a windlass on the beach out to the wreck. Anything detachable and portable was removed and transported back to the landing area by trolleys that ran on narrow railway lines. The ship's crest and bell were taken, as were unbroken bottles of aerated water and hundreds of tins of corned beef, sardines and salmon. Huge condensers and water tanks were dragged ashore, but were left to rust where they lay as they could not be safely removed from the island. The stripped hulk later slipped back off the reef into deeper water.

Two more German cruisers were given the name *Emden*. *Emden III* paid a courtesy call to Cocos in 1927 under the leadership of the first *Emden*'s torpedo officer, Captain Witthoeft. A party of sailors went ashore on North Keeling and placed a wooden cross over the graves of the sailors who had been buried there. The sun-bleached skulls of two original crewmen, which for some bizarre reason graced the foyer of *Oceania House*, were buried at sea with full naval honours.

Between the wars, groups of 20 Cocos Malay workers were stationed on North Keeling for up to two weeks at a time under the direction of John Sydney Clunies-Ross' cousin, Edmund. These parties would live in *atap* long-houses built on the western shores of the lagoon. Once or twice a week they would receive a visit from an estate vessel which would deliver foodstuffs and water and return to Home Island with timber, coconuts and birds.

In 1941 a party of Cocos Malay men were taken on board the visiting English warship, the *Danie*, as part of an inspection trip to North Keeling. There they were surprised to find a hidden cache of 400 drums of Japanese submarine fuel and 700 barrels of diesel. All were hastily punctured and destroyed.

In June 1945 a RAF detachment of three Mosquito aircraft was ordered by special request of Lord Louis Mountbatten to fly a top secret photographic mission from Perth to Cocos and onward to Singapore. The weather deteriorated badly as they crossed the Indian Ocean and poor visibility forced them to fly low over the water. Locating Cocos proved to be like trying to find the proverbial needle in a haystack and the trio were rapidly running out of fuel. Spitfires were sent out from Cocos to search for the latecomers and they managed to find and direct two of them in for a safe landing. The third, A52-606, was preparing to ditch in the ocean when her two crew spied the island of North Keeling. Flight Lieutenant Langsford managed to effect a belly landing on the island and he and Flying Officer Tozer escaped without injury. The seas were too rough to rescue them that night, but they were taken off the following day. Most of the useful components of the wrecked aircraft were later salvaged and utilised as spare parts.

After the death of John Sydney Clunies-Ross in 1944 the frequency of booby-bird hunting trips to North Keeling increased considerably. The earlier rules about the type of birds that could be taken or where they could be taken were overlooked. Groups of *jukongs* would go whenever the weather was suitable and thousands of birds would be brought down with shotguns as well as the traditional flails. Barges would travel to the island once or twice a year to gather coconuts or bring back birds for *Hari Raya* festivities.

In 1950 a Japanese salvage company removed as much of the hull of the *Emden* as they could and shipped the scrap back to Japan. In good weather they utilised a mother ship, a smaller vessel and teams of hard-hat divers. One of these men is believed to have died and been buried on the island.

Nowadays, with local wages being paid in Australian currency, Cocos families are able to save for outboard motors and substantial aluminium boats that can easily handle the 24 km trip to North Keeling. Ironically, these powered craft also possess a greater potential than the old sailing boats for breaking down or speeding past their destination in bad weather. A number of *jukongs* lost their way to Keeling in earlier times, but most eventually made it safely back to port. A missing power-boat necessitates a full-scale search-and-rescue operation, as it has the potential to be so much further afield. Such a search had to be mounted in September 1987 when three wayward bird hunters failed to return home. Four nights and half a million dollars later, they were found alive and well in their tiny dinghy 60 nautical miles to the west of the atoll. By agreement, strict rules and quotas now apply to seabird hunting in the Territory. No birds at all can be taken from North Keeling and organised sports shooting is confined to Horsburgh Island.

Today a visit to North Keeling is only possible in the company of the Government Conservator of Wildlife. Long-term studies of the bird rookeries on the island are currently being conducted to learn more about the breeding patterns and population characteristics of the different species that inhabit the island.

Most of the time this isolated isle is left undisturbed under the watchful eye of its legendary female *penunggu*, or 'guardian'. This spirit is said to live in the area around the landing place and sit atop a large, pedestal-shaped coral boulder on the beach. Since the war years a superstition has grown up that discourages women from visiting the island. Until only the last year or two, no Malay women or girls were permitted to go there. The presence of females was said to annoy the guardian spirit and it was believed that storms or tidal waves would follow any such visits.

These are the major islands in the Cocos-Keeling group. Tiny as they may be, they have nevertheless witnessed a series of human dramas that would rival that of far larger places. Indeed, the story told here resembles a miniature version of the modern history of the world.

Unfortunately, the majority of mainland Australians have yet to hear about these distant Australian atolls. It is hoped that this Bicentennial publication will assist in rectifying the situation. These islands, their people and their history are far too important to remain unrecognised any longer.

Appendix

COCOS (KEELING) ISLANDS — CLIMATIC AVERAGES (based on daily observations since 1901)

	Jan.	Feb.	Mar.	Apr.	May	Jun.	Jul.	Aug.	Sep.	Oct.	Nov.	Dec.	Annual
Mean daily max. temp. (°C) + [highest on record]	29.6 [32.1]	29.9 [32.4]	29.9 [32.1]	29.6 [32.2]	29.2 [31.4]	28.5 [30.7]	28.0 [29.9]	28.0 [29.8]	28.2 [30.0]	28.7 [30.6]	29.0 [31.1]	29.4 [32.2]	29.0 av.
Mean daily min. temp. (°C) + [lowest on record]	24.5 [21.1]	24.8 [20.1]	24.9 [19.8]	24.9 [19.6]	24.7 [19.4]	24.1 [20.1]	23.6 [20.4]	23.5 [18.3]	23.4 [19.0]	23.8 [20.6]	24.1 [19.3]	24.3 [21.1]	24.2 av.
Average no. of days over 30°C	11	13	15	12	5	1	0	0	0	1	3	7	
Mean 9 a.m. relative humidity (%)	75	75	77	78	78	77	78	76	73	72	73	73	75.4 av.
Average rainfall (mm)	205.9	162.6	235.2	251.1	184.9	202.2	201.9	143.1	85.1	74.1	103.1	128.0	1977.2 total
Average no. of rain-days	11	15	17	18	16	17	18	16	12	10	10	11	
Average no. of days thunder is heard	1	1	2	2	1	0	0	0	0	0	0	0	
Average no. of days of strong wind (over 35 km/hr)	2	2	3	3	5	6	10	10	8	5	4	2	
Mean 9 a.m. sea-level air pressure (mb)	1010.9	1010.3	1011.1	1011.4	1011.7	1012.7	1013.1	1013.7	1014.4	1014.2	1012.9	1011.9	

(*Source:* Bureau of Meteorology records)

PERCENTAGE OCCURRENCE OF WIND DIRECTION (9 a.m.)

	Jan.	Feb.	Mar.	Apr.	May	Jun.	Jul.	Aug.	Sep.	Oct.	Nov.	Dec.
CALM	7	8	6	4	2	1	2	2	—	—	1	2
N	4	3	3	1	1	1	1	1	—	1	1	1
NE	4	3	5	4	4	4	5	3	3	3	3	4
E	19	17	25	44	34	36	37	48	47	41	31	20
SE	45	39	41	41	51	49	49	42	47	53	59	61
S	15	15	12	4	7	7	5	4	2	2	4	10
SW	4	5	4	1	1	—	1	—	—	—	1	—
W	2	5	3	1	—	—	—	—	—	—	—	—
NW	1	4	2	1	1	—	—	—	—	—	—	—

(*Source:* Bureau of Meteorology records)

MAXIMUM WIND GUSTS AND DIRECTION (knots)

	Jan.	Feb.	Mar.	Apr.	May	Jun.	Jul.	Aug.	Sep.	Oct.	Nov.	Dec.
Speed	95	66	55	55	54	60	47	70	47	47	78	51
Dir.	W	SW	NNW	E	W	ENE	ESE	W	SE	ESE	NNW	S

(*Source:* Bureau of Meteorology records)

OCCURRENCE OF MAJOR CYCLONES

1862	1893	1909
1876	1902	1968

COCOS (KEELING) ISLANDS — COPRA EXPORTS 1880–1986

Year	Tonnes	Year	Tonnes
1880	500	1948	550
1890	750	1954	550
1893	500	1960	410
1895	800	1965	654
1902	400	1970	182
1908	600	1975	300
1910	000	1980	253
1920	500	1984	160
1935	750	1986	118

Note: The industry ceased to operate in 1987.

Sources: Colonial Office records; Commonwealth Dept of Territories Annual Reports

DE FACTO OWNERS OF THE COCOS (KEELING) ISLANDS, 1826–1978

ALEXANDER HARE
Born: London, 17??
On Cocos: May 1826–1831
Died: Java, 1834

JOHN CLUNIES ROSS
Born: Shetland Islands, August 1786
Married: Elizabeth Dymoke, 1820
On Cocos: February, 1827–1854
Died: Cocos, 1854

JOHN GEORGE CLUNIES ROSS
Born: London, 1823
Married: Supia Dupong, 1841
On Cocos: 1827–1871
Died: Cocos, 1871

GEORGE CLUNIES ROSS
Born: Cocos, 1841
Married: (a) Inin, 1868
       (b) Ayesha, 1895
On Cocos: 1862–1910
Died: Isle of Wight, 1910

JOHN SYDNEY CLUNIES-ROSS
Born: Cocos, 1868
Married: Rose Nash, 1926
On Cocos: 1910–1944
Died: Cocos, 1944

JOHN CECIL CLUNIES-ROSS
Born: London, 1928
Married: Daphne Parkinson, 1951
On Cocos: 1949–1985

CAPTAIN CLUNIES ROSS' PARTY, 1827

J. Clunies Ross, wife and 5 children	7
Mrs Clunies Ross' mother, Mrs Dymoke	1
Anna Andrews (servant maid)	1
10 British seamen as follows:	10
J. B. Gray (apprentice)	
W. C. Leisk (apprentice)	
Andrew Moody (apprentice)	
C. Steevens (apprentice)	
J. Steevens (apprentice)	
R. Steevens (blacksmith)	
Joseph Bayley (carpenter)	
Thomas Deely (carpenter)	
George Brown (tailor & boatman)	
J. Munslaw (boatman)	
Ivan Antonio (cook) Portuguese	1
2 hired native servants	2
Henry Keld (from ship wrecked on West Island, Dec. 1826)	1
	Total 23

ALEXANDER HARE'S PARTY, AS REPORTED IN 1829

H. van der Jagt reported Hare's group to consist of 36 men, 25 women and 37 children (all slaves)	98
Norman Ogilvie (arrived Nov. 1828, supervisor)	1
Alexander Hare	1
	Total 100

Source: Gibson-Hill, Documents, 1952

COCOS (KEELING) ISLANDS — FIRST CENSUS, 15 DECEMBER 1837, TOTAL = 138

Men's names	Women's names	Sons	Daughters	Total
Pa Elling	Ma Elling	1	—	3
Damien	Booroo	2	1	5
Pa Saban	Ma Saban	6	2	10
Gendoot	Amina	2	1	5
Minuet	Ma Booroo	—	1	3
Bassier	Ma Bassier	1	3	6
Pa Jayia	Ma Lyma	1	5	8
Ipaoo	Ialeima	—	1	3
Angoor	Ma Julia	—	1	3
Pa Myle	Ma Myle	3	1	6
Tomas	Ma Lyda	3	2	7
	Ma Boging (widow)	4	2	7
Pa Summah	Ma Summah	6	3	11
Pa Ripa	Ma Juinasn	1	1	4
Pa Kah	Ma Kah	4	1	7
Pa Mera	Ma Mera	—	1	3
Sangray	—	—	—	1
Pa Booro	—	—	—	1
—	Memmae	—	—	1

Aged Persons

	Ma Chews	—	—	1
	Ma Minuet	—	—	1
	Ramping	—	—	1
	Ma Jun	—	—	1
	Ma Selibeak	—	—	1

Peons of Madras

7	4	3	3	17

Domestic Gentoos

3	—	—	—	3

Crew of the 'Harriet'

8	—	2	—	10

Americans

2	—	—	—	2

Ross family

1	1	3	2	7

Source: Census Report 1837, Public Records Office (Admiralty), London

134

COOLIE LABOUR CONTRACT FOR 1888

On this Wednesday 11th April 1888 appeared before me Carel Servaas Hein appointed, by decree of the Governor-General of Netherlands India, dated 23rd March 1887, as temporary substitute of the notary Hendrik Jacobus Meerhaus residing in Batavia, in the presence of the here-after to be named witnesses well known to me: the Native men

Arman apparently 23 years
Atjiep apparently 23 years
Siman apparently 28 years
Moe apparently 23 years
Sarveil apparently 23 years
Samae apparently 25 years
Natjeh apparently 24 years
Gerieng apparently 23 years
Antoenie Menol apparently 30 years
Asmian apparently 23 years
Aman apparently 28 years
Siehen apparently 25 years
Alie apparently 30 years
Hassan apparently 28 years
Alieham apparently 23 years
Arie apparently 25 years
Perier apparently 23 years
Nasiman apparently 24 years

all of them without employment and living in Batavia.

On the one part
and Henry Oldam Foster, Esquire, a merchant living at Batavia acting in this matter as a member and consequently for and in the name of Tidman Balfour and Co established in Batavia, the said firm acting under general power of attorney and consequently for and in the name of George Clunies Ross, merchant and agriculturalist living at the Cocos Islands as per general power of attorney No. 27 dated December 1885 drawn up before the notary Mr Anthony Mangelaar Meertens, then residing in Batavia and witnesses.

On the other part
The appearer on the other part being well known to me the notary, whereas the appearers on the one part have been known to me by the native men Abdul Hamid, Head of the district living in Kampong Klenteng, Batavia and Ahad, coolie-mandoer living at Kampong Petje-bokkan, Batavia, and it has been declared by the appearers to have agreed, after having obtained permission by Government's decree No. 2/c dated 1 February 1888 as follows:-

1. The appearers on the one part are to perform the following work, for the benefit of the Settlement belonging to the principal, the appearer on the other part on the Cocos Islands.

Field Labour
Taking care of cocoa and other fruit trees, plucking and gathering of coconuts and other fruit, and further work which they may be called upon to perform. In case of fire, floods or other catastrophes they are to be desposable all day and night to save, and look after property.

2. If a labourer collects more than 2,400 nuts per week, he shall be paid 1 rupee* for every 100 nuts which he collects in excess of that number.
3. The contractors on the one part bind themselves to leave for the Cocos Islands on or about the 12th of this month.
4. The contractors on the one part have to work 10 hours per day, on behalf of the Settlement of the Contractor on the other part, from 6 to 11 o'clock a.m. and 1 to 6 p.m. but the Contractor on the other part has the power to change the working hours, but not to demand more than 10 hours work per day.
5. The Contractor on the other part has to pay to those on the one part 8 rupees-per month wages, to be paid on the 1st day of each month and may be paid weekly if they so desire. Wages to be paid in Cocos currency.
6. The Contractors on the one part admit having received from the Contractor on the other part an advance of 50 rupees each, which will be deducted from their wages by monthly payments of 2 rupees.
7. On the 3 days, during the so-called *Lebaran* (Malay New Year), the contractors on the one part are not bound to work.
8. The Contractor on the other part has to provide, at his own expense, for sufficient and proper lodging, rice and medical attendance for the Contractors on the one part.

The term of agreement is for 3 years successively dating from the day on which the contract has been signed. On expiry of term of agreement the Contractors on the one part are entitled to free passage to Batavia per one of the vessels belonging to or chartered by the Contractor on the other part. All and everything subject to the habilities fixed by law.

In witness where of this deed done and passed in Batavia in the presence of Johannes Florentinus and Lim Enkway, clerks both living at Batavia as witnesses by whom and also by the appearer on the other part the attesting witnesses and myself the notary, this deed has been signed immediately after the same has been read out and explained in Malay, the other appears not being able to sign their names as not having been taught to write.

The original of this deed has been duly signed and stands written on a one and a half guilder stamp.

Issued as a literal copy

Signed: C.S. Hein

Notary's seal

* Mr Ross informed me this was a mistake on the part of his Agents, the rate should be 1 rupee for every 400 nuts. The men are, I take, entitled to the benefits of their contract, but the question cannot immediately arise, as until they have had at least one year's experience they will not be able to avail themselves of the excess rates.

Source: N. P. Trevenen, Report, 1888, (Straits Settlements Annual Report)

ISLANDER POPULATION, 1874–1903

Year	Cocos Islanders	Bantamese	Total
1874	292	198	490
1880	310	125	435
1885	377	139	516
1886	386	170	556
1887	377	118	495
1888	385	150	535
1889	385	141	526
1890	390	146	536
1891	373	183	556
1892	389	185	574
1893	394	210	604
1894	387	192	579
1895	403	191	594
1897	410	201	611
1898	425	187	612
1899	427	188	615
1901	570	68*	638
1902	550	76*	626
1903	567	71*	638

* children of Bantamese labourers were classed as
Cocos Islanders from 1901 onwards

Source: Smith, 1960

COCOS (KEELING) ISLANDS — INFANT MORTALITY, 1888–1944

Year	No. of Births	No. Deaths before 1 yr	% Surviving to Age 3
1888–92	162	56	64.8
1893–97	176	84	51.1
1898–02	166	61	61.4
1903–07	182	66	61.5
1908–12	153	49	66.7
1913–17	181	34	78.5
1918–22	204	19	85.3
1923–27	234	20	83.8
1928–32	292	24	83.6
1933–37	346	28	85.3
1938–42	383	35	84.1
1943–44	184	21	81.5

Source: Smith, 1960

POPULATION STRUCTURE OF COCOS MALAY POPULATION, 1901–1980

	Age group	Males		Females	
		No.	%	No.	%
1901:	0–4	43	13.1	79	23.0
	5–10	43	13.1	37	10.8
	10–15	25	7.7	40	11.6
	15–20	30	9.1	32	9.3
	20+	186	57.0	156	45.3
1947:	0–4	186	20.6	211	23.4
	5–9	145	16.0	145	16.1
	10–14	102	11.3	126	14.0
	15–19	110	12.2	90	10.0
	20–24	80	8.8	73	8.1
	25–29	74	8.2	57	6.3
	30–34	50	5.5	51	5.7
	35–39	29	3.2	32	3.6
	40–44	35	3.9	31	3.5
	45–49	27	3.0	29	3.2
	50–54	16	1.8	14	1.6
	55–59	17	1.9	17	1.9
	60–64	10	1.1	7	0.8
	65–69	11	1.2	6	0.7
	70+	12	1.3	9	1.0
1970:	0–4	14	6.0	17	6.9
	5–14	72	30.6	69	27.8
	15–49	120	51.0	137	55.2
	50–64	26	11.1	22	8.8
	65+	3	1.3	3	1.2
1975:	0–4	19	7.6	22	8.4
	5–14	45	18.1	51	19.4
	15–49	153	61.5	165	62.6
	50–64	27	10.8	23	8.7
	65+	5	2.0	2	0.8
1980:	0–5	14	10.0	9	6.0
	6–14	19	13.6	24	16.0
	15–49	88	62.8	103	68.7
	50–64	13	9.3	12	8.0
	65+	6	4.3	2	1.3

Sources: Smith, 1960; Commonwealth Dept. of
Territories Annual Reports

Note: fully detailed population records are
currently unavailable to researchers

COCOS (KEELING) ISLANDS — OVERALL POPULATION STRUCTURE, 30 JUNE 1986

Age	Males				Females			
	Home Is.		West Is.		Home Is.		West Is.	
	No.	%	No.	%	No.	%	No.	%
0–14	56	28.2	42	33.6	58	27.0	57	41.6
15–49	114	57.3	74	59.2	126	58.6	68	49.6
50–64	14	7.0	9	7.2	17	7.9	12	8.8
65–75+	15	7.5	0	0.0	14	6.5	0	0.0
Totals:	199		125		215		137	

Home Island: 199 Males + 215 Females = 414 people
West Island: 125 Males + 137 Females = 262 people
Grand Total: 676 people

Source: Commonwealth Dept. of Territories Annual
Report for the Cocos (Keeling) Islands

POPULATION OF HOME ISLAND, 1830–1960

Population

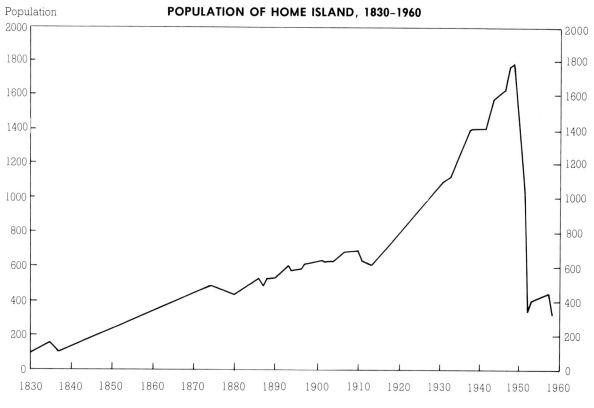

POPULATION OF THE COCOS (KEELING) ISLANDS, 1960–1986

Population

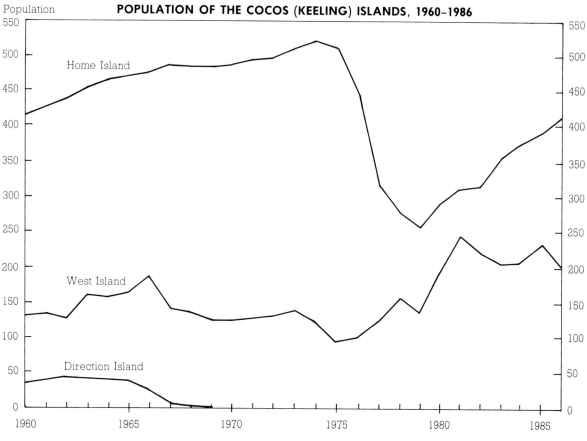

Home Island

West Island

Direction Island

COCOS MALAY NAMING SYSTEM

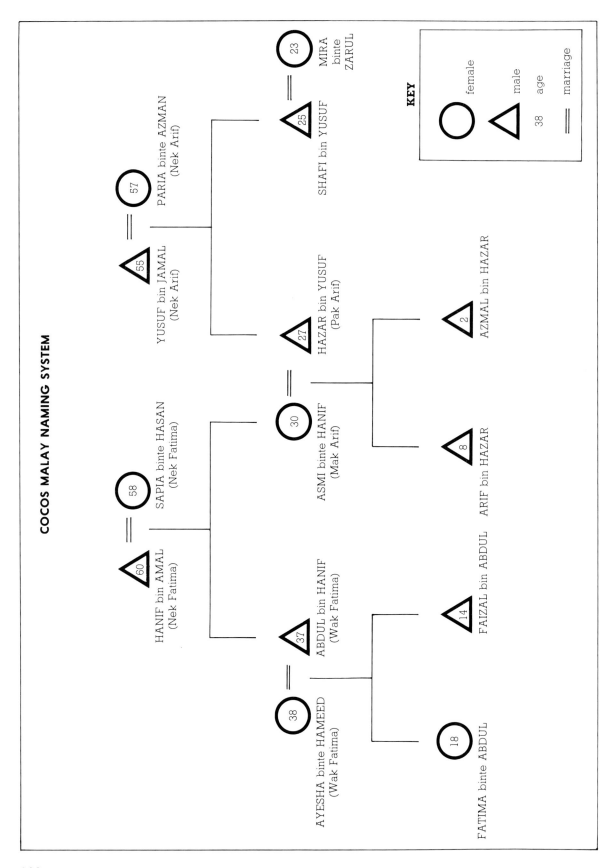

KEY

◯ female

△ male

38 age

═ marriage

COCOS MALAY NAMES AND FORMS OF ADDRESS

Cocos Malay children are given just one name at birth (*nama muda*) and modes of address change as a person rises in family and social status. It is impolite to refer to adults by their childhood name. People prefer their status-names (*nama kampong*). There is a formal code of etiquette and politeness when referring to people.

LEGAL NAMES

Males	**Abdul**	**bin**	**Hanif**
	(given name)	(son of)	(father's name)

Females	**Asmi**	**binte**	**Hanif**
	(given name)	(daughter of)	(father's name)

Women do not take their husband's name on marriage, but retain their own legal name. As a result, three different 'surnames' may occur within the one family:

Husband: Hanif bin Amal
Wife: Faridah binte Hasan
Son: Abdul bin Hanif
Daughter: Asmi binte Hanif

The husband in this family should be addressed as 'Mr Hanif' or 'Mr Hanif Amal' *not* as 'Mr Amal'. That is his father. To save confusion on the mainland, ex-Cocos women consent to using their husband's 'surname' as their own, ie., 'Mrs Faridah Amal'. This still does not solve the problem of children having a different 'surname' to their father.

FAMILY STATUS NAMES

Husband's Name:	**Hanif**
After 1st child:	**Pak Abdul**
Senior status:	**Wak Abdul**
After 1st grandchild	**Nek Fatima**

Wife's Name:	**Sapia**
After 1st child:	**Mak Abdul**
Senior status:	**Wak Abdul**
After 1st grandchild:	**Nek Fatima**

Senior status is accorded to parents of children of marriageable age, those in positions of responsibility and those to whom respect is due.

INTERPERSONAL REFERENCES

When Cocos Malay people speak to each other, they constantly acknowledge each other's status in relation to their own.

Note: The 'a' sound in each of the following terms is 'a' as in 'father'. A final 'k' is not sounded; it is a glottal stop.

child to mother: *mak*
child to father: *pak*
adults/parents to a child: *nak* (short for *anak*)
younger child to older brother/older male cousin/older male friend: *bang* (short, for *abang*)
wife to husband: *bang* (short for *abang*)
younger child to older sister/older female cousin/older female friend: *kak* (short for *kakak*)
older child to younger sibling/friend: *dik* (short for *adik*)
addressing a grandparent: *nek* (short for *nenek*)
grandparent addressing grandchild/child young enough to be a grandchild: *cuk* (short for *cucuk*)
addressing a close aunt/ uncle: *wak*
addressing a distant aunt/ adult female: *bik* (short for *bibik*)
addressing a distant uncle/ adult male: *man* (short for *paman*)

COCOS (KEELING) ISLANDS — SCHOOL ENROLMENTS, 30 JUNE 1988

	Home Island School		West Island School			
	Boys	Girls	Boys		Girls	
			Home Is.	West Is.	Home Is.	West Is.
Year level						
12			1	0	1	1
11			2	0	1	1
10			3	3	5	4
9			1	1	4	1
8			5	1	3	5
7	3	3	2		3	
6	5	1	1		3	
5	4	4	2		3	
4	0	4	3		1	
3	8	6	3		2	
2	6	1	4		5	
1	7	6	1		4	
Pre-Primary	6	7	4		1	
Play Group	2	5	3		4	
Totals	41	37	12	28	14	38

Source: School Records

Bibliography

Australian Electoral Commission, *Cocos (Keeling) Islands Act of Self Determination*, Australian Government Publishing Service, Canberra (1984)

Bunce, P., *Cocos Malay Culture*, Commonwealth Dept. of Territories, (1987)

Cogger, H., Sadlier, R., Cameron, E., *The Terrestrial Reptiles of Australia's Island Territories*, Australian National Parks and Wildlife Service, Canberra, (1983)

Covacevich, J., "The Cocos Islands", *Wildlife in Australia*, March 1983, pp. 6–9.

Crusz, N., *A World War II Mutiny on Keeling-Cocos Islands (1942)*, M.A. Thesis, University of NSW, (1979)

Darwin, C., *On the Structure and Distribution of Coral Reefs*, Ward Lock, London, (1890); *A Naturalist's Voyage Around the World*, John Murray, London, (1906)

Forbes, H., *A Naturalist's Wanderings in the Eastern Archipelago*, Sampson Row, London, (1885)

Gibson-Hill, C. A., "Notes on the Cocos (Keeling) Islands", *Jnl. Mal. Br. Roy. Asiat. Soc.*, 20(2), 1947, pp. 140–202; "The Island of North Keeling", *Jnl. Mal. Br. Roy. Asiat. Soc.*, 21(1), 1948, pp. 68–103; "The Birds of the Cocos (Keeling) Islands", *Ibis*, 91, 1949, pp. 221–143; "Documents Relating to J. Clunies-Ross, Alexander Hare and the Establishment of the Colony on the Cocos (Keeling) Islands", *Jnl. Mal. Br. Roy. Asiat. Soc.*, 25(4 and 5), 1952.

Guppy, H. B., "The Cocos Keeling Islands", *Scot. Geog. Mag.*, 5(6), 5(9), 5(11), 1889.

Holman, J., *Voyage Around the World*, Vol. 4, p. 371, Smith, Elder & Co., London (1835).

Hoyt, E. P., *The Last Cruise of the* Emden, Andre Deutsch, London (1967).

Hughes, J., *Kings of the Cocos*, Methuen and Co., London (1950).

Jacobson, G., "Preliminary Investigation of Groundwater Resources, Cocos (Keeling) Islands", *Bureau Mineral Resources Record* Melbourne, 1976/64 (unpublished).

Laten, S., Rabika, K., Kabul, M. N., 'Sejarah Dan Kebudayaan Suku Cocos', *Malaysia in History*, 16(2), Kuala Lumpur, Dec. 1973.

Mullen, K., *Cocos Keeling — Islands Time Forgot*, Angus and Robertson, Sydney (1974).

Parliamentary Papers No. 183, *A Report on UN Involvement with Australia's Territories*, Australian Government Publishing Service, Canberra (1976).

Rees, C. and L., *Westward From Cocos*, G. G. Harrap, London (1956).

Slocum, J., *Sailing Alone Around the World*, Granada, London (1900).

Smith, T. E., "The Cocos-Keeling Islands: A Demographic Laboratory", *Population Studies*, London, 14 Nov. 1960.

Stokes, T., Sheils, W., Dunn, K., "Birds of the Cocos (Keeling) Islands, Indian Ocean", *Emu*, Melbourne 1984.

Tarling, N., 'The Annexation of the Cocos (Keeling) Islands', *Historical Studies*, Melbourne, 8 May 1959.

Van Der Wat, D., *The Last Corsair*, Hodder & Stoughton, Australia (1983).

Wood-Jones, F., *Corals and Atolls*, Lovell Reeve, London (1910).

Index

Note: Page numbers in *italics* indicate an illustration.

144